"For Many Shall Come In My Name"

How mainstream America is accepting the "Ancient Wisdom" teaching and what this foreshadows.

by
Ray Yungen

Revised Edition

Solid Rock Books, Inc.
979 Young Street • Woodburn, Oregon 97071

Cover design / production assistance by
Clint Crittenden, **Words Unlimited** • Woodburn, Oregon

Contents

Introduction

In January of 1984, an event occurred which changed my life. John, a good friend of mine, began telling me about a book entitled *Hidden Dangers of the Rainbow*, which was alerting the Christian community to something called "the New Age movement." He was very excited and insisted I read it as soon as possible.

At first I thought *Hidden Dangers* sounded like a crackpot book written by someone who was making a mountain out of a molehill. Consequently, I didn't read the book thoroughly—only what interested me. But my gleaning sparked a desire to know more about this "New Age" belief system and what its proponents were saying.

My curiosity grew as I began to check things out for myself. I combed through health food stores and New Age book stores looking through books, pamphlets, and magazines. It became obvious to me that what *Hidden Dangers* was saying *did* have some validity. There definitely was something significant going on which I had not fully grasped before. As the scope of my research widened, I realized that the New Age movement is a larger phenomenon than most people perceived.

It wasn't long before I encountered detractors who thought I was wasting my time, or worse, delving into areas which were dangerous. Despite this criticism, I remained staunchly convinced of the validity of my pursuit. I examined my motives and seriously considered whether or not the research I was doing was legitimate. After much self-examination, I came to the conclusion that my research should continue because what I was doing would someday benefit other people (New Agers very much included). Many shocking, progressive revelations occurred over the next few years. Society was, indeed, being affected on a grand scale.

My research had a beneficial side effect. It sparked in me a deeper spiritual interest, which seems logical when one considers the implications of the New Age movement. I have been a believing Christian since the age of nine, but for the most part, I had been a passive, "worldly" one rather than one who "earnestly contends for the faith." I knew a few Bible verses and was not greatly committed to learning more. I always felt convicted about my apathy but never acted on that conviction. Now, though, I felt I was really onto something. How could I continue to remain indifferent?

I began giving presentations to small groups of interested people. I documented these talks with the material I had collected, comparing this material with various Bible verses that I felt challenged New Age assertions.

In the fall of 1986, a supporter requested that I compile my research into a packet of information. Books have been written on this subject from a conservative Christian viewpoint, but he wanted something short, simple, and packed with the information I had shared with him personally.

At the time of his request, I had acquired so much material that something "short and simple" was going to be highly impractical if I wanted to relate the full picture of what I had learned. It was then that I decided to write a book.

This book is not meant to be a detailed in-depth study

of the New Age movement. It is meant to be a concise, compact sketch that will give the reader a clearer understanding of what the New Age movement entails. I have documented my research and presented the facts for your benefit. My hope is that it will tie together certain links you may not have understood before reading *For Many Shall Come In My Name.*

Ray Yungen
1991

CHAPTER 1

What is the New Age?

My first exposure to what I later came to know as the New Age movement was in 1974 when I moved to Berkeley, California, to attend a film institute. From the first day I arrived, I found "Berserkeley" (as it was nick-named) to be a fascinating and exotic town, a place unlike any I had ever seen. The town surged with a rebellious, wacky vitality. It has been said of Berkeley that the strange and the odd are ordinary and the conventional out of place.

Berkeley had a notorious reputation as a hotbed of student protest dating from the Free Speech movement in 1964. I lived only a few blocks away from the vacant lot called "People's Park", which was the scene of bloody clashes between police, street people, and students in 1969. Militant Leftist rhetoric and literature were in evidence everywhere. Telephone poles displayed various manifestos and communiques from groups with formidable sounding names such as "the People's Revolutionary Underground Red Guerrilla Commune." Pictures of Chairman Mao and Karl Marx decorated the walls of several co-op health food stores.

There was also a very open and prevalent drug culture. Smoking pot in public was so common that it was taken for granted. I was familiar with the drug culture and radical politics through personal exposure and the media, but it soon became apparent that there was something else happening in Berkeley that I had not encountered before.

NEW TERMINOLOGY

Many unfamiliar terms began to catch my attention. I met people who talked about such things as "karma" and "exploring inner space." I frequently heard the words *aquarius* and *aquarian*, and it was commonplace to ask about a person's "sign."

I noticed that many of those who were using these terms were not burned-out street people but rather the articulate and well-educated. Their unusual spiritual outlook intrigued me, but I passed it off as the eccentricity associated with Berkeley and the San Francisco Bay area. Had someone told me this "aquarian consciousness" would someday spread through every facet of Western society, I would have thought them as crazy as the wild-looking street people hanging around the periphery of the University of California.

FAMILIAR WORDS - NEW DEFINITIONS

While living in the Berkeley Film House I became friends with Brian, a young man from the East Coast. Brian was personable, intelligent, and witty. With both of us being avid film buffs we enjoyed many good times together discussing the cinema, and even made plans to collaborate on a film someday.

After I had completed my film courses, Brian offered to drive me home to Oregon in his rattletrap Volkswagen bug so he could check out the beauty of the Northwest. Eventually, he settled in a city near my hometown enabling us to keep in touch.

During our visits, Brian often talked about subjects

he termed *spiritual* or *holistic*. Often he spoke about Christ or "Christ consciousness" and the world peace and brotherhood which would eventually be achieved through this. It all sounded very positive.

Each time these sermons took place, I wondered just what it was he was trying to convey. The words he used were familiar, but the meanings he attached to them were peculiar and out of place. The exchanges I had with Brian were very frustrating at times.

Whenever I tried to present a more traditional Christian viewpoint on spiritual matters, he would become highly irritated and respond with, "The Bible is nothing but metaphor to show deeper spiritual truths" or "the churches have completely missed the real meaning of Jesus' teachings and have substituted rigid rules and dogma to control people instead." Brian was adamant on this belief.

What perplexed me was how Brian had developed these spiritual ideas which he had tried so hard to make me understand. He didn't belong to a cult or anything of that sort. I wondered where these ideas came from. I would ask him, "Brian, what *is* this?" He would shoot back, "You can't label truth."

Although I didn't see it clearly at the time, Brian's spiritual outlook was a mixture of what he referred to as, "*All* the world's great spiritual traditions and paths." He talked about Jesus and often quoted from the Bible, yet he had a little shrine in his apartment to the Hindu mystic and saint Sri Ramakrishna. He genuinely felt there was *no difference* between the teachings of Jesus and Ramakrishna. "The great masters all taught the same thing—the kingdom of God is *within*," he would declare with great conviction.

WHAT IS THE NEW AGE MOVEMENT?

In the last twenty years, a curious spiritual movement has increasingly made itself known in the Western world. It is collectively referred to, both by its adherents and its foes, as the New Age movement. Only in recent years has it come out into the open and moved into the mainstream of society.

One New Age writer put it quite accurately when he observed the following:

> It has been going on for decades —probably, by some people's definitions, for centuries—and yet there can be no denying that it has now taken on a new sense of exponential growth that suggests it could well touch the lives of everyone on the planet by the year 2000.[1]

An accurate definition of the New Age movement would be: Individuals who, in the context of historical occultism, are in mystical contact with unseen sources and dimensions; receive guidance and direction from these dimensions; and who *promote* this state-of-being to the rest of humanity.

It is extremely difficult to understand this movement without first understanding the underlying belief systems and practices that accompany its agenda. Equally necessary is an understanding of where these beliefs and practices originated and how they have become pervasive.

THE AGE OF AQUARIUS

The term "New Age" is based on astrology. Those who believe in astrology believe there are cosmic cycles called "Astrological Ages," in which Earth passes through a cycle or time period when it is under the influence of a certain sign of the zodiac. These "Ages" last approximately 2,000 years, with a "cusp" or transitory period between each.

Those who embrace astrology say that for the last 2,000 years we have been in the sign of "Pisces," the fish. Now they say we are moving into the sign of "Aquarius" or the "Age of Aquarius," hence the "New Age."

The Aquarian Age is supposed to signify that the human race is now entering a "Golden Age." Many occultists have long heralded the Aquarian Age as an event that would be significant to humanity. That is why one New Age writer stated that "a basic knowledge of Astrological Ages is of enormous importance in occult work."[2]

They believe that during these transitions certain cosmic influences begin to flow into the mass consciousness of mankind and cause changes to occur in accordance with the spiritual keynote or theme of that particular Age. This phenomenon is known as "planetary transformation"—an event they believe will bring "universal oneness" to all mankind. The view is that as more and more members of the human race "attune" themselves to "Aquarian energies," the dynamics of the "old age" will begin to fade out.

Just what "energies" are we supposed to be attuning ourselves to? New Age thought teaches that everything that exists, seen or unseen, is made up of energy—tiny particles of vibrating energy, atoms, molecules, protons, etc. All is energy. That energy, they believe, is God, and therefore, *all is God.* They believe that since we are all part of this "God-energy," then *we, too, are God.* God is not seen as a Being that dwells in heaven, but as the universe itself. According to one writer, "Simply put, God functions in you, through you, and as you."[3]

The Age of Aquarius is when we are all supposed to come to the *understanding that man is God.* As one New Age writer put it, "A major theme of Aquarius is that *God is within.* The goal in the Age of Aquarius will be *how to bring this idea into meaningful reality.*"[4]

METAPHYSICS

To fully comprehend the above concept, one has to understand its *essence* which is built on a belief system commonly referred to as *metaphysics.* The word translates as meta—"above" or "beyond," and physical—"the seen" or "material" world. So metaphysics relates to that which exists or is real, *but is unseen.* The *Dictionary of Mysticism* describes metaphysics as "a science dealing with intelligent forces or unknown powers."[5]

Although the word *metaphysics* is used in non-New Age connotations, it is used in reference to the occult arts so often that the two have become interchangeable. From now on, when I use the term *metaphysics*, I am referring to *New Age* metaphysics.

Metaphysics concerns itself with the spiritual evolution of the human soul. This is called the "law of rebirth," more commonly known as *reincarnation.*

Metaphysics teaches that there is the seen world known as the physical or material plane, and the unseen world with its many different planes. They teach the "astral" plane is where people go after death to await their next incarnation or bodily state.

Metaphysical thought holds the view that we are constantly caught up in a cycle of coming from the astral plane, being born, living, dying, and returning to the astral existence. They believe that the reason for repeating this cycle is to learn lessons that are necessary for our evolutionary training.

The Earth plane is supposed to be the ultimate school. If a person "flunks" one incarnation, he must make up for it in the next cycle. This is called "the law of karma." Reincarnation and karma are always linked together as there cannot be one without the other. Ultimately there is no evil, only lessons to be learned.

What is the main lesson? That *you* are God. This is *the* basic tenet of metaphysical thought. How does one go about "learning" this? How is this perception achieved?

MEDITATION

The ultimate goal in metaphysics is attuning oneself to "higher consciousness" thereby gaining an awareness of these higher worlds or realms. It is taught that the most direct way to achieve this is through the practice of *meditation*. Meditation is the basic activity that underlies *all* metaphysics and is the primary source of spiritual direction for the New Age person. We need only observe the emphasis which is placed on meditation to see the importance of it in New Age thought.

> Meditation is the doorway between
> worlds...the pathway between dimen-
> sions...[6]

> Meditation is the key—the *indispens-*
> *able* key—to the highest states of aware-
> ness...[7]

> Meditation is a key ingredient to
> metaphysics, as it is the single most
> important act in a believer's life.[8]

What exactly *is* meditation? The meditation many of
us are familiar with involves a deep, continuous *thinking*
about something. But New Age meditation does just the
opposite. It involves ridding oneself of all thoughts in
order to "still" the mind by putting it in pause or neutral.
An analogy would be turning a fast-moving stream into a
still pond by damming the free flow of water. This is the
purpose of New Age meditation. It *holds back* active
thought and causes a *shift* in consciousness. The following explanation makes this process very clear:

> One starts by silencing the mind-for
> many, this is not easy, but when the mind
> has become silent and still, it is then pos-
> sible for the Divine Force to descend and
> enter into the receptive individual. First it
> trickles in, and later, in it comes in waves.
>   It is both transforming and cleansing;
> and it is through this force that divine
> transformation will be achieved.[9]

This condition is not to be confused with "daydreaming," where your mind dwells on a *subject.* The way New Age meditation works is that an *object* acts as a holding mechanism until the mind becomes thoughtless, empty—silent.

When this state is achieved some remarkable and convincing experiences can result. One woman described hers in the following way:

> In 1984, when I first learned to meditate, I had read that prayer is talking to God and meditation is listening, so I opened my mind and listened without realizing that meditation is a powerful force. Soon I began to notice unusual sensations in my body while meditating. It felt like energy flowing through me....Gradually the sensations became stronger and after a while it seemed like electric currents were coursing through my body. My fingers tingled and I felt a slight throbbing in the palms of my hands.[10]

The two most common methods used to induce this "thoughtless" state are *breathing exercises,* where attention is focused on the breath, and a *mantra,* which is a repeated word or phrase. The basic process is to focus and maintain concentration without thinking about what you are focusing on. Repetition on the focused object is what triggers the blank mind.

Just consider the word *mantra.* The translation from

the Sanskritt is *man*, meaning "to think", and *tra*, meaning "to be liberated from."[11] Thus, the word means "to be freed from thought." By repeating the mantra, either out loud or silently, the word or phrase begins to lose any meaning it once had. The same is true with rhythmic breathing. One gradually tunes out his conscious thinking process until an altered state of consciousness comes over him.

I recall watching a martial arts class where the instructor clapped his hands once every three seconds as the students sat in meditation. The sound of the clap acted the same as the breath or a mantra would—something to focus their attention on to stop the active mind.

Other methods of meditation involve drumming, dancing, and chanting. This *percussion-sound* meditation is perhaps the most common form for producing trance states in the African, North/South American Indian, and Brazilian spiritist traditions. In the Islamic world, the Sufi Mystic Brotherhoods have gained a reputation for chanting and ritual dancing. They are known as the *Whirling Dervishes*. Indian Guru, Rajneesh, developed a form of active meditation called *dynamic meditation* which combines the percussion sound, jumping, and rhythmic breathing.

THE HIGHER SELF

At the very core of the meditation effort is the concept of what is called the *Higher Self*. This is thought to be the part of the individual linked to the "Divine Essence" of the Universe, the part of man that is "God." It is contact with this Higher Self that is the ultimate goal in meditation and has always been at the very heart of occultism.

There are many different names for the Higher Self, including: the *Oversoul, True Self, Real Self, Inner Self, Core Self, Inner Teacher, Inner Guide, Inner Light, Inner Essence, Inner Source, Inner Healer, Soul-Self, Inner Wisdom, Christ Self, Superconscious, Divine Center, Divine Spark, Atman,* and the *Creative/Intuitive Self.* Any name that smacks of some latent source of "inner knowledge" or "mystical power" can be used.

As stated earlier, the goal of meditation is to *subdue* the conscious or active mind so that higher consciousness can enter. The metaphysician believes that if he can connect himself *to* and eventually attune *with* his Higher Self, this will facilitate the Higher Self's emergence into the physical plane bringing the person under the guidance and direction of this source. This connection is referred to in New Age circles as *awakening, transformation, enlightenment, Self-realization, Cosmic consciousness, Christ consciousness, nirvana, satori,* and finding "the kingdom within."

New Agers believe the person has been "asleep" as to who he is and why he is here through all of his previous incarnations. Once the person discovers and joins up with his "divine presence," he "awakens" from his lower-self sleep state.

They believe that once a person knows the "truth" about himself, he no longer has to come back to the Earth plane anymore. Having learned that he is "God," he rises after death into the higher planes as pure spirit, up the cosmic evolutionary ladder where there is no limit to how far he can evolve. Once this state has been reached he can then act as a *spirit guide* for those further down the ladder by giving them advice while they are in meditation.

Also, once a person merges with the Higher Self, he is on his way to what they call *empowerment*. This means that one is capable of creating his or her own reality. They claim all power is within the Higher Self, so when one is in tune with it he can run his own show. Fear of creating bad karma is supposed to keep one from using this power for evil purposes.

Metaphysicians believe that we all create our own circumstances anyway, so when one is guided and empowered by the Higher Self, one can consciously "co-create" with it.

The technique used for this is called *creative visualization*. Author Diane Stein explains the link between meditation and visualization in *The Women's Spirituality Book*. She first instructs her readers to do the rhythmic breathing and deep relaxation exercises (meditation), a prerequisite for entering "the receptive state" and "going between the worlds."[12] Stein then gives an example:

> A woman wishes to hold a seashell in her hand. She visualizes the shell she desires, its shape, texture, what it feels like to hold, its color and salty odor. If she continues this visualization nightly, she soon finds her seashell. Someone brings the shell to her from their beach vacation, she sees and buys it at a garage sale or finds it long forgotten in her own basement. When she sees the shell, she recognizes it immediately as her own. Her

desire is fulfilled, the thought form trans-
ferred to the physical level, the object
itself drawn to her from between the
worlds.[13]

Another explanation of how the creative visualization
process works is offered by John Randolf Price in his
book, *The Super Beings*:

Say you want a new home. A new
house will not suddenly appear in the
back yard of your present dwelling.
Events and circumstances will take place
enabling you to acquire the home you
desire.[14]

Meditation and creative visualization definitely
accompany one another in this process. As one New Age
manual explained: "Tune in to the Inner Divinity, the
Source, the God within, and feel that Presence as you.
This first step is essential. If it is incomplete, the rest of
the process will not work."[15]

MANIFESTATIONS

Upon examination of New Age materials, it becomes
quite apparent that even though they claim that the Higher
Self is within you, there is *a visible presence*. These
beings can be seen at times, such as the following con-
firms:

Your Higher-Self can appear to you in
many forms, depending on what you need

at a particular time. Some people report experiencing their Higher-Self as specifically male or female. But more often, people report perceiving their Higher-Self as a being of light which seems beyond sexuality—beyond the physical separation between male and female.[16]

Shirley MacLaine described her "Higher Self" in the following profound encounter:

> I saw the form of a very tall, overpoweringly confident, almost androgynous human being. A graceful, folded, cream-colored garment flowed over a figure seven feet tall, with long arms resting calmly at its side. It raised its arms in outstretched welcome....It was simple, but so powerful that it seemed to "know" all there was to know....'Who are you?' I asked....The being smiled at me and embraced me! 'I am your higher unlimited self,' it said.[17]

This reflects the "geni in the lamp" story popularized by cartoons and a television sit-com of the 1960's. Originally the geni represented the Higher Self, who was reached through meditation by staring at the flame of an oil lamp. It was believed that a person could have whatever he or she wanted, once in touch with it.

Our word "genius" comes from this latin word for spirit guide and now means a person with great creative power.

THE ULTIMATE REALITY

To review, the New Age concepts of "Self-realization" are:

- All that exists *is* God.
- All Mankind is *part* of that divinity.
- In each person there dwells the Higher Self which is the *divine essence* of that person.
- The Higher Self is the guide to realizing the wisdom of the universe.
- Meditation (stilling the mind of thought) is the way to connect with the Higher Self.
- A person can control his own reality once he has contacted the Higher Self, working in unison with its powers.

These fundamental elements I've just stated are indicative of the New Age. This phenomenon is more than just an intellectual acceptance of *ideas*. There has to be a real power or force involved to give *seeming validity* to these belief structures. To believe one is God one must first *feel* like he or she is God.

As one teacher of these practices commented:

> We try to help people get in touch with their divine self or their inner self, whatever one wants to call it. It's not religious, it's spiritual. It's connecting with that divine being within yourself or whatever you want to call it and acknowledg-

ing the power you have, the control you
have over your life. You're not out of control. You are not helpless.[18]

I have often wondered why the "spooky" nature of
metaphysics has not detered more people from becoming
involved in it. Its appeal comes from the way it is presented.

The following incident clearly shows how metaphysics is viewed by its adherents. I was browsing
through a New Age bookstore with a couple of friends.
Before long they began quietly muttering to each other
their disapproval of what they were seeing. The owner of
the store overheard their remarks and in an incredulous
and irritated voice asked them, "What's the matter, don't
you want to *grow*?"

When Oprah Winfrey featured Shirley MacLaine on
her April 11, 1989 talk show, it was obvious that they
both shared this belief when Winfrey promised her TV
viewers that if they embraced MacLaine's methods and
ideas they would be "healthier, happier, and have peace of
mind." In relation to New Age metaphysics Winfrey told
MacLaine, "I'm trying to help everybody get it."

New Agers see what they are involved in as nothing
more than self-development and emancipation from the
bonds of life's frustrations and failures. They believe they
are in touch with a source that will *improve* their lot in
life and bring them personal happiness and well-being.

A perfect example of this viewpoint is found in the
spiritual quest of Celeste Graham. Graham was a remarkably talented and accomplished young lady. By the age of
sixteen she managed her own record company and maga-

zine and at seventeen went on to have her own publishing house. She also attained three doctorates and numerous degrees along the way.

What she lacked, though, was a sense of understanding of why she was here, and why all her material accomplishments didn't end her soul-searching and frustration with life? Soon Graham became involved with meditation and metaphysics. For Christians, or anyone else, to fully understand why the New Age movement has become so popular, they must first understand the sense of elated discovery that is propelling huge numbers toward the same direction as Graham, who proclaimed:

> God-conscious awareness, or awakening to our divinity is the ultimate freedom. It opens doors to experiences that are beyond our imagination. It elevates man to his highest estate, frees him from the limitations of the physical, and lifts him up to the divine. It is the purpose of life, the ultimate reality.[19]

CHAPTER 2

The Advent of the "Ancient Wisdom"

Many people may think the New Age movement is a collection of strange cults populated by aging hippies, emotional cripples, and assorted oddballs who are being duped by money-hungry charlatans and egocentric frauds. This may be true in some instances, but if such were the overall case, I would not have spent the last seven years researching this movement or writing about my discoveries. The focus of this book is not on "fringe" religious groups or New Age "riff-raff" but a broad-based effort to influence and restructure our *whole society*.

Rather than creating new institutions, as is the case with cults, the New Age goal is to transform the people within existing institutions and thereby transform the *institutions themselves!* As one writer explained it, "...a *new* society forming within the heart of the old."[1]

This transformation has frequently been referred to as a *paradigm shift*. The word *paradigm* means "model," as in outlook or viewpoint.

New Agers predict that as more and more people achieve contact and guidance from the Higher Self, this will eventually translate into a *global shift* in which the transformed state will become as common as watching television or reading a newspaper. It will be the predominant model or paradigm for humanity.

The New Age movement is very diverse and offers an intriguing array of "spiritual paths" that promise enlightenment and wholeness. Anyone seeking to "expand their consciousness" has varying options for accomplishing their desire. By examining and understanding the New Age, a person discovers that there is a path suited to every taste and personality, from the most outrageous to the most respectable and seemingly scientific.

How large is the New Age movement? It's impossible to ascertain an accurate count since not all New Agers belong to organized groups. Finding an accurate number also depends on the definition of who is a New Ager. Tens of millions believe in reincarnation, including 23 percent of all Americans.[2] However, many of these are not as yet engaged in meditation.

A 1978 Gallop Poll indicated that 10 million Americans were engaged in Eastern meditation that year. A book published in 1975 entitled *Spiritual Awakening* listed 8,000 New Age organizations in the United States at that time.[3] The numbers are even greater today.

New Age leader Barbara Marx Hubbard, who was placed in nomination for Vice President of the United States in the 1984 national election, stated she could "bring in 15 to 20 million 'spiritually-based' people for the Democratic ticket."[4]

These figures correlate with the research Stanford Research Institute (SRI) has conducted. They estimate the number of New Agers in America could be as high as 5 to 10 percent of the population—12 million or more people.[5]

THE MYSTERY SCHOOLS

Many people have a kind of bemused contempt for those involved with mysticism, and thus, they believe that the New Age movement is a frivolous frolic into the absurd.

In answer to this I would like to emphasize two points. First, millions of people are having *real experiences*. Second, these experiences are as old as human civilization.

It is important to understand that the foundation which the New Age movement is based upon transcends mere intellectual acceptance of ideas. It cannot be seen as separate from the mystical experience from which it springs.

The Mystery Schools are the most easily documented of the ancient adherents of occultism. They were the caretakers of this esoteric knowledge.

These schools formed the nucleus of the religious practices of ancient nations and empires such as Egypt, China, Chaldea, Persia, Greece, and Rome, as well as the Aztec and Inca civilizations.

The Mystery religions were so labeled because their teachings were kept hidden from the common people. In fact, the term occult originated from the Mystery religions because the majority of the people were ignorant of their true meanings. The priests and adepts (who were initiated through various grades or levels) were the ones who gained insight into these hidden "truths" of the universe.

What was it that was kept hidden or secret? It can best be summed up as the knowledge of the *laws and forces* that underlie the universe but are not evident to the five senses of man's normal perception. Basically they taught an awareness of the invisible worlds for wisdom and guidance; and the development of psychic abilities and spiritual "healing" techniques.

The core teachings of occultism are often referred to as "the Ancient Wisdom" by New Age writers. They also refer to it as "the Secret Wisdom," "Ageless Wisdom," and "the Perennial Wisdom." Many believe this Ancient Wisdom can be traced back to the fabled civilization of Atlantis.

Despite enormous geographical distances and cultural differences, "the Mysteries" all taught the same message: "Happy and blessed one, you have become divine instead of mortal."[6]

THE THEOSOPHICAL SOCIETY

If one were to mark any particular beginning of the modern New Age movement, it would have to be the founding of the Theosophical Society in 1875. *Theos* is the Greek word for "God" and *sophos* is the Greek word for "wisdom." The Theosophical Society was to be the society for the study of "the wisdom of the Divine."

The Society was started in New York City by Helena Petrovna Blavatsky, a Russian noblewoman, and Col. Henry Olcott, an American occultist.

The main purpose of Theosophy, as it was called, was to open the door for occult teachings to spread throughout Western society. It concentrated on the development of *occult powers* within the individual rather than concerning itself simply with contacting the dead as did the spiritualist movement. The core of Theosophy can best be explained by the following statement:

> Our Theosophical teachers have all
> repeated the old, old doctrine as the fun-
> damental on which to build—the doctrine
> that the real human being is not the poor
> weak creature he too often thinks he is,
> and exhibits to others, but a wondrous
> *spiritual Being* in the innermost recesses
> of his nature, a divine mystery, and that it
> is within his power, and indeed it is his
> destiny, to realize this and eventually
> become it.[7]

Madame Blavatsky, or HPB as she was known, was
one of the most illustrious figures of modern occultism.
She inspired thousands of people all over the world to
embrace the Ancient Wisdom. The publicity that sur-
rounded her fueled this interest to a large degree. The following story is typical of the way she would respond to
those that doubted the validity of the Theosophical philosophy:

> At a party, she materialized a cup and
> saucer. Outraged by suggestions that she
> might have planted them, she asked her
> hostess if there was anything she particu-
> larly wanted. The hostess mentioned a
> brooch she had lost some years before.
> After communicating with her 'masters,'
> HPB announced that it was buried in a
> flower bed. The company trooped outside,
> dug among the flowers, and promptly
> found the brooch.[8]

Although Theosophy's influence has greatly waned, Theosophical lodges can still be found around the world. The Theosophical Society was instrumental in beginning what is now known as the New Age movement.

ALICE ANN BAILEY

In the early twentieth century, a figure who would have a major impact upon the western esoteric movement came out of Theosophy. The popularization of the very name "New Age" has been attributed to her writings. Her name was Alice Ann Bailey.

Born Alice LaTrobe-Bateman in Manchester, England, on June 16, 1880, she grew up as a society girl and enjoyed all the privileges of the British upper-class. Alice, being very religious, met and married a man who later became an Episcopal minister. In time they moved to the United States.

When Alice's husband physically abused her, she left him and settled with her three children in Pacific Grove, California. She was greatly comforted when she met two other English women living in Pacific Grove. These women introduced her to Theosophy, which seemed to provide answers to Alice's questions concerning why such misfortune had befallen her. Alice, then thirty-five, was about to have her life changed forever.[9] Later on, in her unfinished autobiography, she wrote:

> I discovered, first of all, that there is a great and divine Plan....I discovered, for a second thing, that there are Those Who are responsible for the working out of that

Plan and Who, step by step and stage by stage, have led mankind on down the centuries.[10]

In 1917, Alice moved to Los Angeles and began working for that plan at the Theosophical headquarters where she met Foster Bailey, a man who had devoted his life to the Ancient Wisdom. She divorced her husband and married Bailey in 1920.

Alice had her first contact with a voice that claimed to be a master in November of 1919. Calling himself the "Tibetan," he wanted Alice to take dictation from him. Concerning this Alice wrote, "....I heard a voice which said, 'There are some books which it is desired should be written for the public. You can write them. Will you do so?'"[11]

Alice felt reluctant at first to take on such an unusual endeavor but the voice continued urging her to write the books. Alice experienced a brief period of anxiety in which she feared for her health and sanity. She was finally reassured by one of her other masters that she had nothing to fear and that she would be doing a "really valuable piece of work."[12]

The "valuable work" Alice was to do lasted thirty years. Between 1919 and 1949, by means of telepathic communication, Alice Bailey wrote nineteen books for her unseen mentor.

To occultists, the significance of the Alice Bailey writings was that they heralded the appearance of a "World Healer and Saviour" in the coming Aquarian Age that would restore the teachings of the Mystery Schools and unite all mankind under his guidance.[13]

This "Coming One," who she called "The Christ," was not the Lord Jesus Christ whom Christians await the return of, but an entirely different individual. This man was to embody all the great principles of occultism, chiefly the *divinity and perfectibility of man.*

A TARGETED GENERATION

Prior to the late 1960's, occultism in America was relatively obscure and considered to be an eccentric pursuit. If such ideas were discussed in public, the person expressing them would have been considered to be "peculiar."

The 1960's changed all that in a relatively short period of time. I remember once having a conversation with an older lady who had been involved with occultism all of her life. She recounted to me how New Age thought "hadn't really gotten anywhere until the hippies came along, then things really started to get off the ground." Her observation could not have been more accurate.

Many people think of the 1960's as a time when a bunch of outlandish young people acted up and tweaked the nose of "straight" society. In reality, it was a social and cultural revolution of gigantic proportion. These shifts of attitudes during the 1960's deeply affected the social fabric of the entire Western world.

The youth/drug/rock counterculture, as it was called, could be broken down into three basic segments:

The Radical Political Element. Collectively known as "the New Left," they wanted to "off the pig" (kill police), "smash the state," and give "power to the people." In other words, they considered themselves to be the politically motivated vanguard which would lead "progressive" elements of society in a broad-based socialist revolt against what they perceived as the "capitalist/imperialist coalition" of government and the military. In addition to those who wanted revolution there were many who simply wanted peace in Vietnam.

The Hedonists. These were the ones who really just wanted to party. This meant getting stoned, engaging in promiscuous sex, listening to Jimi Hendrix or the Jefferson Airplane, looking hip, and giving lip service to whatever seemed to be fashionable at the time. They had no real commitment to anything other than their own pleasure.

The Spiritual Seekers. These were the ones who had spiritual insights from their involvement in drugs (mainly LSD) and Eastern mystical practices. They were into yoga, I Ching, tarot cards, astrology, Zen, Native American lifestyles, Atlantis, UFOs, ESP, Eastern gurus, reincarnation, holistic health, and other such interests. In other words, instead of Marxism and pleasure seeking, these people were delving into the Ancient Wisdom as the answer to the world's problems. What made them significant is that they numbered in the *millions.*

A book called *The Starseed Transmissions,* purportedly channeled from a being who calls himself "Raphael," has been received in New Age circles as a book to be taken seriously. Many highly respected New Age leaders, such as Jean Houston, have praised it for telling us what the intention and plan of the New Age is really all about. The book gives some keen insights. In it, Raphael describes the mission he and his kind are pursuing:

> There is but the flimsiest of screens
> between your present condition and your
> true nature. It is our mission to assist you
> in bridging this gap, to awaken you from
> sleep, to bring you to the fulfillment of
> destiny.[14]

According to Raphael, the 1960's played a key role in this mission. This is very apparent in his comments about that time period. He speaks of their first large scale entry into our "historical process" in the late 1960's:

> At that time, the members of your
> species most responsive to our descend-
> ing vibrational patterns were those who
> had not yet assumed clearly defined social
> roles. Within them, we could plant the
> seeds of our Life-giving information with
> the greatest chance for successful germi-
> nation....We chose the years 1967 to 1969
> for this first large scale experiment,
> because at that time in your global civi-
> lization there was an entire generation
> coming into maturity that was receptive to
> change on a planetary scale.[15]

What Raphael said he and his kind were going to do *has happened* just the way he explained it would. The generation that embraced these metaphysical ideas in the 1960's has been the catalyst for the current surge of spiri-tual transformation that is now permeating our society. Because of this, occultism is no longer a proper term for the Ancient Wisdom since it is *not* hidden from view or kept secret any more. In fact, just the *opposite* is now the case. Being anything *but* hidden, it is highly visible and available to anyone. I heard one practitioner put it very aptly: "In the last twenty years occultism has come out of the closet and it will *never* be driven back in again." Another metaphysician made a similar concurrence by stating:

> At one time such cosmic knowledge was hard to come by. It was known as the mystery teachings, or the occult (hidden) teachings, or the secret doctrine and it was only available to selected individuals in secret retreats which have always existed on Earth. Now it is available to all who are interested.[16]

THE NEW AGE AROUND THE WORLD

The New Age phenomenon is by no means confined only to America. In virtually every country in the world you can find evidence that it is having an impact. In countries such as India, Japan, and Nigeria, it has been the traditional spirituality for centuries. In many others, especially countries that have been traditionally Christian, the New Age movement is expanding. West Germany is a good example of this. Consider the following quotes from a West German magazine:

> [The movement] has exploded in the
> BRD (West Germany) - [since] 1986 an
> infrastructure has spread out...it is very
> typical of the early phases of a mass
> movement...Germany is over-ripe for
> New Age," says Gerd Gerken of the
> Creative House. "In this country there is a
> high potential for the transformation."[17]

Great Britain has also been engulfed in the New Age
tide. One annual New Age festival in London draws a
crowd of 70,000 or more.[18] A sympathetic English clergy-
man had this to say:

> The popularity of the Meditation
> movement today is beyond doubt. All sec-
> tions of society, religious and secular,
> urban and rural have felt its impact. It is
> everywhere apparent, from the now famil-
> iar groups meeting regularly in church
> halls for the practice of Yoga to the recent
> invasion of rural Sussex by Budhist con-
> templatives.[19]

Even the Soviet Union has a thriving interest in
Aquarian pursuits. A book on citizen diplomacy to the
Soviet Union revealed:

> Growing numbers of Soviets are
> experimenting with and avidly pursuing
> interests in meditation, yoga, vegetarian-
> ism, exercise, massage, encounter groups,

gestalt groups, est, underwater birthings, crystals, psychic healing, clairvoyance, telepathy, Aikido and transformational-ism....Literature on yoga, sufism, Budhism, Vedanta, Cabala, the lost knowledge of ancient civilizations, and other esoteric subjects is available and finds a wide audience...we know for certain that many top officials are involved in these activities themselves.[20]

I have also come across indications that many other countries are heavily involved. Australia's New Age movement is very active. I once counted over 300 groups and organizations listed in the back of an Australian New Age magazine. Brazil is another major stronghold with approximately 60 million adults (nearly half of the entire population) involved in spiritist religions.[21] In Poland, where it is called *Nowy Wiek*, the movement is spreading fast.

The Ancient Wisdom established a foothold with the mass following in the 1960's, consolidated its position in the 1970's and is making a major push around the world. You can encounter it anywhere if you know what to look for.

RELIGION OR SCIENCE?

In the last twenty years many groups and individuals have come forward with various "psycho-technologies" for maximizing *personal growth* and *human potential*—this potential being in the Higher Self. New

Agers understand metaphysics must be presented in a way that will attract the greatest number of people—the advantage being that those who might reject any perceived attempts to slip them religion of any kind, would find the idea of "growth techniques" acceptable. Maharishi Mahesh Yogi did this with his Transcendental Meditation program emphasizing "the Science of Creative Intelligence" rather than mantra yoga which is what it really is. Others have promoted scientific sounding terms like "alpha state awareness" or "intuition development" which are just imaginative names for meditation.

The advantage New Agers have in enacting significant change in our society is evident in the following quote: "Metaphysics can be taught in highly religious terms, or it can be taught as a *pure science, without any religious connotations whatsoever*" (italics mine).[22]

When metaphysics is presented as a science, it is possible for a person to not be aware of its spiritual influence. Many people now coming into direct contact with the Ancient Wisdom do not realize, nor understand, what it's all about. They may be told it concerns the latest findings on "human development," since many times the people presenting it do not want them to know the true nature of it. The goal is to merge these practices into society so they will be considered normal and acceptable. To accomplish this they change terms; meditation becomes "centering" and the Higher Self may be called anything that sounds positive. The key is to rename any terminology that might turn people off. A metaphysics teacher once boasted to me that, "All I have to do is drop the mystical connotations and businessmen *eat this stuff up. The experience sells itself.*"

The following example illustrates this point well: I was talking once with the owner of a New Age bookstore when I noticed she had the hard-core material (i.e., channeling, spirit guides, etc.) located toward the back of the store, while the more mainstream books (i.e., self-help, holistic health, transpersonal psychology, etc.) were up in front. I made the comment that there was really no difference between the two since they were both based on opening yourself up to the power of the Higher Self. The owner's face broke into an impish grin and, putting her index finger over her lips in a "hush" gesture, she replied, "I know, but don't tell anybody."

A SUBTLE EFFORT

I know of another store in a major West Coast city that sells books, tapes, and videos on "stress reduction." An entire room is devoted to posting fliers and brochures on metaphysical workshops and seminars in the area.

The owners are very active in their community. Doctors, therapists, and teachers come to them for help. They have given talks to school faculties, major corporations, all the major hospitals in their city, churches, service organizations, and senior citizen groups. Their clientele tends to be affluent, well-educated professionals and business people who are interested in "personal growth."

They emphasize such seemingly beneficial endeavors as stress reduction and self-improvement with an additional element added—*spiritual awareness*. One of them related how she attended a powerful workshop with "Lazaris" and discovered his techniques were practical and usable. That doesn't sound too extraordinary until you find out that Lazaris is not a person but a *spirit guide.* Considering the possible nature of that workshop, listen to what a brochure on Lazaris had to say:

> There will be several incredible Guided Meditations and the very touching Blendings with Lazaris. A Blending is when Lazaris combines his energy with ours to touch us individually either to impart knowledge into our Subconscious or to help us create the reality we desire. The Blendings are very intimate times to just be with Lazaris.[23]

Because of our stereotypes of people who previously gravitated toward mystical experiences (such as counter-culture types), we may tend to assume that people associated with the New Age movement are odd-looking, have strange personalities, or are in other ways "offbeat." The two owners I have just described are very bright, articulate, well-dressed, and above all, *extremely personable.*

A newspaper reporter who did an article on one of them informed me that she was "one of the most calm, serene persons I have ever met." The reporter added, *"People want what she has."*

I wonder what she would have said had she known this "serenity" was probably the result of "Blendings" with a spirit guide and that this woman was promoting the same state-of-being to others on a wide scale.

MISSIONS TO ACCOMPLISH

Those involved in the New Age movement do not work by accident or coincidence. Rather, they have a mission to accomplish and receive "inner guidance" to show them where, when, and how that work must be done. A woman I am acquainted with told me about a situation that happened to her. One evening a stranger began chatting with her. She had never met him, yet he told her things about her early life that he had *no possible way of knowing*. The accuracy of his information about her past greatly disturbed her. The man then explained why he had approached her. He said he had been "sent" to "save" her and that he was guided to her by a "central source of wisdom," and told her that she, too, could get in touch with that *same source*. He promised her that once she had connected with it she could have anything she wanted in life. Greatly unnerved, she quickly departed from his company.

In the book and TV miniseries, *Out On a Limb* by Shirley MacLaine, the character of David Manning is seen in the role of an Aquarian conspirator. Throughout the book, he influences MacLaine, slowly but surely, to get deeper and deeper into metaphysics. Finally he reveals the motive of his interest in her: "What it comes down to, Shirley, is that you're to be a teacher, like me, but on a much wider scale."[24] If she was to be a teacher, then there had to be someone who wanted her to teach—to be her "overseer" so to speak. New Age writer, David Spangler, makes it clear who these overseers are and what they want. Referring to his own spirit guide, "John," he wrote:

Over the years it has been evident that
John's main interest is the emergence of a
new age and a new culture, and he identifies himself as one of those on the spiritual side of life whose work is specifically
to empower that emergence.[25]

We must conclude then that there are *no real leaders
in the New Age movement, only followers."* I heard one
writer/channeler put it very plainly when he revealed:
"Everyone anywhere who tunes into the Higher Self
becomes part of the transformation. Their lives then
become orchestrated from other realms."[26] This aspect
has to be understood in order to fully grasp the significance of the New Age movement.

It may appear on the surface that all of these groups
and individuals are not connected, but the following quote
sheds light on the real situation. One New Age writer
confirmed:

Soon it also became apparent that
those of us experiencing this inner contact
were instinctively (and spontaneously)
drawing together, forming a network. In
the many years since, I have watched this
network grow and widen to literally
encompass the globe. What was once a
rare experience—that of meeting another
person who admitted to a similar superconscious presence in his or her life—has
now become a common, even frequent,
event...what I once saw as a personal (and

individual) transformation I now see as
part of a *massive and collective human
movement* (italics mine).[27]

In his extremely revealing and insightful book, *The
Emerging New Age*, sociologist J.L. Simmons disclosed
that there are, in essence, "tens of thousands" of metaphysical teachers and counselors in America today who
are in the process of training and guiding "hundreds of
thousands" of students and clients. In addition to these,
there are "millions" who have "a sporadic but real interest" in metaphysics.

Simmons observed that "Each of these circles is
growing in numbers. And there is a steady progression of
people inward: an uncommitted person moves into the
active, part-time circle, and so on."[28]

Simmons also related that because of this swell of
interest the movement was "doubling in size every three
to five years."[29] The Ancient Wisdom isn't just for cave-
dwelling mystics anymore!

CHAPTER 3

The New Age In Business

If there was one single group to whom the promise of creating one's own reality would have specific appeal, it would be business people. The competition in the corporate world is so keen that anything, no matter how unusual, would be eagerly embraced if it offered results. As they say in the business world, the "bottom line" is success.

The way New Age thought has crept into corporations is simple to understand. Management trainers and human resource developers hold positions where they can incorporate metaphysics into business under titles such as "Intuition Development," "Right Brain Creativity," and "Superlearning."

The New Age Journal stated:

> An unconventional new breed of consultant has surfaced on the corporate lecture circuit. They speak of meditation, energy flow and tapping into the unused potential of the mind. What's more, they are spreading their Arcane curriculum not only among the alternative entrepreneurs who populate the capitalist fringe, but within the heart of corporate America as well. General Electric, IBM, Shell, Polaroid, and the Chase Manhattan Bank

are sending their fast-trackers to crash
courses in, strange as it may sound, intuition.[1]

Once, while attending a New Age convention, I was
told by one of these "new breeds" that resistance to New
Age concepts in business was being replaced by a *new
openness*. "How you focus it is all important," he
explained. "If you barge in with occult lingo it turns them
off right away. You have to tell them how you can make
their employees happier and get more productivity out of
them—then they will listen. You are *really* teaching metaphysics, but you present it as *human development*."

THE QUIET REVOLUTION

This approach has tremendous appeal because compa-
nies naturally want to get the most out of their people.
New Agers know this approach works to their advantage.
One trainer defined her role the following way:

There is something new in the fact
that businesses are taking an active interest in the potential of these techniques to
bring about transformational change within large groups of people for organiza-
tional ends. You have to deal with the
whole person—body, mind and spirit—if
real change is to happen."[2]

In a 1983 interview, New Age writer Marilyn
Ferguson echoed the same theme:

Business leaders have, by and large, exhausted materialistic values and are often open to *spiritual* values....What's more, top-level business people are not afraid of the transformation process, and typically, after I speak to them, they say, 'I didn't know that such things were possible? I don't understand everything you're saying, but I'm going to find out about it.' Whereas most people who don't understand new concepts automatically reject them, business people, who by nature are trained in risk taking, go after them.[3]

Dennis T. Jaffe, Ph.D., founder and director of the Learning for Health Clinic in Los Angeles, had this to say:

Many progressive companies are incorporating some of the inner directed exercises [meditation, visualization] into their 'manual of procedures'....These changes point to a quiet, inner-directed revolution that is reshaping many companies into being *agents of self-realization*...Many social thinkers, such as Marilyn Ferguson, believe that because of its openness to change, business has the greatest potential for spiritualizing the world (italics mine).[4]

A number of courses, books and individuals are having a great impact on the business world. The following are some examples: Michael Ray and Rochelle Myers have written a book entitled *Creativity in Business*. The book is based on a Stanford University course that they claim has "revolutionized the art of success."[5] Two people who enthusiastically endorse this book are Spencer Johnson, M.D., coauthor of *The One Minute Manager*, and Tom Peters, coauthor of *In Search of Excellence*. Another one, Silicon Valley Bank Chairman, N.W. Medearis, says the book is "an experience which will leave one significantly changed."[6]

Ray and Myers acknowledge that the book "takes much of its inspiration from Eastern philosophy, mysticism and meditation techniques" and that "dozens of America's brightest and most successful business practitioners and entrepreneurs have contributed to the course and this book."[7] It is absolutely amazing how unabashed this book is in its presentation of metaphysics as a source of creativity.

In one section we find the heading, "Getting in Touch with Your Inner Guide." It says, "In this exercise you meet your wisdom-keeper or spirit guide—an inner person who can be with you in life, someone to whom you can turn for guidance."[8] The way one contacts these beings is by breathing or mantra meditation. If there is any doubt the book is talking about New Age meditation, it is resolved upon reading: "As meditation master Swami Muktananda says, 'We do not meditate just to relax a little and experience some peace. We meditate to unfold our inner being."[9] Tarot cards are even presented as a source of creativity. As with other New Age categories, it begins with breathing exercises (or as the book says, "...go into silence"). The person then picks the cards which are supposed to give "some important insights."[10]

Twenty years ago some of the methods *Creativity in Business* endorses would have been scoffed at—but not today. Now there is an openness to try anything that might work. If this book was just an isolated situation, it could be easily dismissed as a flash in the pan, but it is not.

Two others who apply New Age techniques to business are Craig R. Hickman and Michael A. Silva, authors of *Creating Excellence: Managing Corporate Culture , Strategy and Change in the New Age.* In the preface of their book, Hickman and Silva state:

> We have written *Creating Excellence* to teach people the practical skills they must acquire before they can become the sort of leaders we call New Age executives."[11]

These practical skills would sound appealing to almost anyone in a position of leadership and responsibility. Hickman and Silva say that the "art of meditation" is the key to mastering the skills of creative insight and focus. They relate:

> Intense meditation helps you attain the state of mind that *lets* your sometimes hidden inner reserve of knowledge and experience float to a conscious level. Like most of the hundreds of executives we've trained, you may at first resist meditation

as a frivolous undertaking, but if you give
it a chance you'll probably discover
knowledge you didn't know you pos-
sessed.[12]

This is a typical approach. You will recall an earlier
quote, "businessmen eat this stuff up, the experience sells
itself." That is why it is making such headway, it works.
The back cover of the paperback edition of *Creating
Excellence* has the following endorsement from
Boardroom Reports which states: "Tells what it takes to
get to the top of the executive ladder and remain there." If
these methods work for people in business today the way
they worked for Madame Blavatsky in finding the woman's lost brooch related in Chapter 2, then it's easy to see
the implications of metaphysics on the business world.

REINVENTING THE WORLD

Another person actively applying New Age techniques to business is John Naisbitt. His book,
Megatrends, sold *six million* copies and made him a voice
to be heard. Newsweek magazine stated:

Currently the author receives around
20 to 30 requests a day to share his vision
of the future with trade and corporation
chiefs around the world.[13]

According to the article, Naisbitt and his wife,
Aberdene, are both active in the New Age arena. They
meditate together for twenty minutes each day, believe in
reincarnation and have a "spiritual advisor" who gives

them "life readings." This article also told of a meeting in Telluride, Colorado, over which Naisbitt and his wife presided. To the 200 "New Age thinkers" who showed up at this conference, Naisbitt declared that the whole world needed to be reinvented. At the top of the list was business.

Following *Megatrends*, Naisbitt and his wife coauthored *Reinventing the Corporation: Transforming Your Job and Your Company for the New Information Society*. In a chapter entitled "The Skills of the New Information Society," Naisbitt conveys how "American companies are discovering the benefits of meditation." He gives examples of companies such as General Motors, AT&T, Adolph Coors Company, and Ampex Corporation that teach meditation to their employees.[14]

Naisbitt says, "Developing creativity means learning how to be at home in these strange new settings." He quotes Dr. Tom B. Roberts, a professor of educational psychology at Northern Illinois University. "We will ultimately define the fully educated person as one who can select the appropriate state of consciousness for his/her purpose, voluntarily enter it, and use and develop the abilities that reside there."[15]

Such enthusiasm, such high praise is especially significant considering that this praise is from a man who is in such incredible demand to share his "vision of the future" with business executives around the world.

CORPORATE "WELLNESS"

"Creativity" is not the only New Age avenue into the corporate scene. Health and fitness programs presented in

the context of "corporate wellness" are becoming increasingly popular. Executives give a willing ear to ways of
keeping productivity up and absenteeism down.

Many of these programs have metaphysical motives
within them. One such "wellness expert" promoting "total
health" explained how she was able to teach mantra meditation to a group of businessmen:

> Just yesterday I met with a whole
> room of executives for breakfast—top
> executives in a huge multinational compa-
> ny...Here were these executives closing
> their eyes and breathing deeply into their
> abdomens, and quieting their mind by
> repeating just one word—"relax, relax."[16]

Earlier in the interview this woman related how she
had "studied metaphysics" and "meditated three or four
times a day for direction."

In her joy at being able to subtly introduce meditation
to those who would have rejected it as being too "far out"
otherwise, she commented: "Ten years ago in an
American company I would have been thrown out in the
street, I'm sure."[17]

BUSINESS - THE MOST LOGICAL CANDIDATE

The New Age effort to transform business is *very
real* and becoming *more successful*. When asked in an
interview about where he thought the vanguard of transformation was in the country today, New Ager James
Fadiman replied:

What's fascinating to me is that when
I met recently with some of the old timers
in the movement, I discovered that all of
us had expanded from working in growth
centers to working in American business.
What the business community needs,
wants, and appreciates at this time are
insights in the human potential movement. I'm finding executives who 20 years
ago considered the human potential movement a kind of joke and who are now
recruiting specialists into the most conservative industries.[18]

Larry Wilson, founder of Wilson Learning
Corporation (one of America's largest management trainers), and coauthor of *The One Minute Sales Person*, clearly stated that metaphysics is the core of what is being
taught.

The heart of our new management
training represents a return to the *ancient
spiritual wisdom about the true identity
and power of the individual*. In our courses, we aim to empower people so they can
get in touch with their creative Source and
then apply the potential to every part of
their lives, including their work life (italics mine).[19]

Wilson also reveals in the interview that it is the
"higher self" that is at the heart of this "ancient spiritual

wisdom." He explains, "Once a sufficient number of employees get in touch with their true potential, the organization changes," and that "it helps to have top management in tune with it."[20] He had the following to say about business' readiness to pursue these concepts:

> The exciting message we're getting is that many businesses are indeed ready. They're sending people to our courses in ever larger numbers. And that's exciting because I believe business is the most logical candidate to lead the significant changes starting to take place in our society.[21]

In an interview, New Age leader Willis Harmon acknowledged that:

> Some of the most creative and successful people in business are really part of this new paradigm movement. You can find this sort of talk going on in business. In fact, a group of business executives and myself got together and created something we call the World Business Academy, which is a network of business executives who have already gone through their own personal transformations to a considerable extent and are asking: 'What's the new role of business? What's the new corporation?'[22]

The March 1991 issue of International Management magazine revealed that many of the major European corporations are also eagerly embracing New Age spirituality. Included in the list were the Bank of England and the UK's Ministry of Defense and Cabinet Office.

One European New Age business consultant proudly remarked: "The revolution of the 1990's will be in seminars and trainings like ours,...there is a major shift going on."[23]

The previously mentioned individuals, and numerous others like them, are working diligently within the corporate world, to bring about a paradigm shift of potentially staggering proportions. Larry Wilson acknowledged this by saying, "This new approach is changing the corporation, and that change will affect other institutions of our society."[24]

New Agers know that if they can transform business, *they will have transformed the world.*

CHAPTER 4

The New Age In Education

The field of education presents an ideal setting for transformation. In virtually every area of education and instruction, from kindergarten to universities, from weekend workshops to family counseling session, the Ancient Wisdom is being taught either up front or covertly. The basic reason for this is that many teachers, principals, and other administrators have become involved in metaphysics. Marilyn Ferguson acknowledged, "Of the Aquarian Conspirators surveyed, more were involved in education than in any other single category of work. They were teachers, administrators, policy makers, educational psychologists."[1]

These people, according to Ferguson, have already begun to attempt significant changes in the educational system. She states:

> Subtle forces are at work, factors you are not likely to see in banner headlines. For example, tens of thousands of classroom teachers, educational consultants and psychologists, counselors, administrators, researchers, and faculty members in colleges of education have been among the millions engaged in *personal transformations*. They have only recently

begun to link regionally and nationally, to
share strategies, to conspire for the teaching of all they most value: freedom, high
expectations, awareness, patterns, connec-
tions, creativity. They are eager to share
their discoveries with those colleagues
ready to listen.[2]

New Age education consists of "developing" the
whole person—body, mind, and spirit—with an emphasis
on the spirit. Often this is termed as *holistic* or *transpersonal* education.

INNOVATIVE TECHNIQUES

A good example of this effort is the work of Jack
Canfield, president of *Self-Esteem Seminars* and former
director of the Institute for Holistic Education. Over the
past sixteen years, he has instructed 36,000 people in his
seminars. In addition, he has trained hundreds of psychologists and counselors and has conducted in-service seminars for over 200 schools and school districts.[3]

In a 1981 interview with *Science of Mind magazine*,
Canfield stated, "The purpose of New Age education is to
help people manifest and express that essential Self."[4]
This is apparent in his self-esteem programs. In the program's *Life Purpose Exercise*, you are supposed to
"access your inner wisdom and find answers to your
questions and solutions to your problems."[5] These exercises use what is referred to as the "closed eye process."
There can be little doubt that this is nothing more than
standard meditation.

In the interview, Canfield presented his strategy for imparting these approaches into the public school system:

> If we point out to educators that they have an 'essence' that can be invoked through 'meditation' and 'centering' exercises, they'll be put off by the buzzwords. But if we give them an experience that leaves them feeling better about themselves and each other, we can move them slowly into more and more internal states of consciousness.[6]

Meditation can be concealed and brought into classrooms without administrators or principals realizing it. I was involved in a situation where a young boy came home saying that his teacher was teaching meditation to his class. His parents called me and explained the matter. I talked with the boy and with an assistant teacher who knew the boy's teacher and concluded that she was involved in either the Shamanic or Wiccan (witchcraft) aspect of New Age consciousness.

After making certain that our concerns were valid, the boy's mother and I went to see the school principal. We were not attempting to get the teacher fired or even to have her reprimanded. We simply asked that her meditation efforts cease in the classroom. The principal thought the boy's mother and I were "needlessly alarmed" and assured us that "nothing of that sort is being taught in this school district."

The principal might have been more concerned if he had read *The Centering Book: Awareness Activities for*

Children, Parents and Teachers by Gay Hendricks and Russell Wills. This book could be called a handbook for the New Age teacher. It says that since meditation and visualization are innovative techniques, the teacher may encounter trouble from school authorities when they are used in the classroom. As Jack Canfield said, it is sometimes expedient to change the terms. The book suggests that "quiet time" or just plain "relaxation" can be used as easily as meditation or centering. It adds that if school authorities object, they should be told these exercises are "promoting relaxed alertness, building positive self-images, and enhancing creativity."[7]

The principal of the school finally asked the teacher to end her meditation efforts, mainly due to his desire to avoid controversy. He condescendingly referred to us as "witch hunters." I think he would be surprised at how close to the truth he really was with that remark.

ONE TEACHERS "WORK"

The following example concerns a public school teacher involved with metaphysics who has self-published a small booklet entitled *Attuning to Inner Guidance*. Her flier also claims that she trains other teachers how to "create a peaceable lifestyle in and out of school and ease anxiety, focus concentration, and apply superlearning concepts."

In her booklet she explains how she became involved in New Age consciousness. She suffered chronic physical pain in her left shoulder from a ski injury. When orthodox medicine failed to relieve her, she turned to alternative therapies for relief. One of them was Reiki, a New

Age healing technique that will be discussed in more detail in the next chapter. As a result of her contact with Reiki, she had a transformation experience. She added, "What a Guide that shoulder was."[8]

Under the heading "Listening Deeply Within" the teacher presents her journal of channelings from her "Inner Teacher" (or Higher Self). The most revealing aspect of this journal is referred to as "My Work." Her Inner Teacher instructs her: "Do not have concern. It is all happening. Make intuitional development [meditation] and Inner Guidance [direction by the Higher Self] commonplace. Get it out there for the everyman [sic]." He then admonishes her to "stay clear and as open as I am."[9]

I obtained a flier with the heading *Parenting With Hope, Health and Humor* presented by community school counselors and child development specialists. The event was held at a local high school on March 10, 1984. I found the teacher who wrote *Attuning to Inner Guidance* listed on the program under "Coping With Family Stress."

People have related stories to me of the influence of other such teachers in the most remote, rural, and conservative of places. A friend of mine who attended a high school in an isolated desert town with a population of less than 350, told me about a science teacher who encouraged his biology classes to "focus on their energy centers" and meditate. Outside of class, he gave her his personal copies of several New Age books. He *truly believed* in the power of these activities and wanted to share them with his students.

COMMUNITY COLLEGE "ASHRAM"

One day I was on my way to a community college library when I happened to see a woman I knew doing her homework in a study area. I walked over and began chatting with her. As we talked, I noticed the large paperback textbook she was using. It was entitled *Becoming a Master Student*. I was curious and asked her if I could look through the book.

The book was crammed with metaphysical concepts. In bold, blue letters it said, "YOU CREATE IT ALL," then explained, "Nothing in the world exists at all except as you create in your head. You create everything."[10]

This is the classic occult idea that we create our own reality, that all is illusion and that true reality can be found only in higher consciousness. In further reading, *I found the pitch.*

Under the heading "Meditation and How To Do It" the book explains that meditation provides deeper relaxation, restores energy, promotes self-healing and that "you can learn a lot from yourself" while in meditation.

It says in order to listen to yourself, you must first pay attention to your breathing and "clear your mind" by repeating a "mantra" or staring at a candle flame and recommends: "Each time a thought enters, gently let it go. Another thought will soon enter. Let it float away."[11] The book also suggested that the student explore and experiment with alternatives such as "psychic healing," which is explained as "effecting cures by focusing spiritual energy."[12] The Personal Development Bibliography offers a list of New Age books which include three by Carlos Casteneda and one by Bhagwan Shree Rajneesh.

The author also lists several teachers who assisted him with their writings. Included were Werner Earhard, founder of est, and Ken Keyes, author of *Handbook to Higher Consciousness.*

When I realized what the book was about, I informed the woman that she had signed up for a course in the Ancient Wisdom. She told me that the other students were eagerly accepting what was being taught in this class.

I know there were many useful ideas in *Becoming a Master Student*, but there is no doubt that the author has an underlying spiritual motive in what he conveys. He is certainly involved in metaphysics, just as the instructors of that class must be.

This community college also featured a place called the "Relaxation Lab" where students could come to relieve "test anxiety." Many teachers on campus were actively promoting this activity and some were even giving their students a choice of doing a paper or going to the "lab." Most students opted for the latter.

When I went to this center to investigate the possibility of metaphysical content I found it right off the bat. Sitting on the receptionist's table were the business cards of the two New Age book stores located in town. The books in the waiting area were *all* metaphysical in nature as were most of the tapes that were used in the "lab."

When I left I wondered how a modern American community college could become, essentially, an "Ashram," or hindu school for meditation, without anyone, except the New Agers, knowing it.

BEYOND THE TRADITIONAL CLASSROOM

The traditional classroom is not the only place a person can receive instruction these days. The past twenty years have seen a tremendous rise in the *workshop* and *seminar* phenomenon. Many of these are conducted within corporations and institutions while others are held independently in hotel or motel conference rooms, community centers, and church or office recreation rooms.

In the last five years of my research I have seen countless brochures, pamphlets, and fliers promoting every conceivable type of New Age seminar.

One promised to "give you the tools with which to fashion the life of your choosing, a life with new goals, new horizons, a new feeling of confidence and self-respect." Such promotions are full of expressions such as "your latent power," "your vast potential," or "the power of your inner being."

Without exception, those who attend these events are promised deep satisfaction, prosperity, and health. The words and style may vary, but what they actually get are nothing more than courses in meditation.

The Learning Annex is a nationwide educational organization offering "short term inexpensive courses to the public." Their headquarters are in New York City, and they also have outlets in numerous other large cities. I found many interesting and practical courses in their catalog such as "How to Start Your Own Business" and "Increasing Your Listening Skills." However, I also found plenty of metaphysics. Offered under "Personal Growth" were courses on past lives, auras, astrology, and self-hypnosis. In one course, "How To Get A Good Night's

Sleep," "ancient yoga technology" (meaning meditation) was presented as the answer. Another one, "An Introduction to Channeling," referred to channeling (having spirits speak through you) as "a tremendously powerful tool of information gathering, self-growth and life enrichment for everyone."[13]

Since education shapes and molds the minds of the world, its potential for bringing about the paradigm shift is phenomenal. With this fact in mind, New Agers are trying to accomplish this in a subtle, yet effective, way.

CHAPTER 5

Holistic Healing

The term *holistic* (also spelled "wholistic") means "body, mind and spirit." In other words, it includes the makeup of the *whole* person. According to this perspective, to achieve optimal health and well-being, all three aspects of the person have to be working smoothly. If one aspect is out of balance, the whole human machine is out of balance. Holistic health practitioners claim their job is to restore balance between the physical, mental, and spiritual elements of their patients. One holistic health source explains: "All agree that the healing is for body, mind, and spirit, and that physical healing is only an entry point for higher spiritual teachings."[1]

Expanding in popularity from the late 1960's, the holistic health field has also been referred to as the *alternative* health movement. In the past, holistic practitioners have tended to be "counterculture" types. Books and catalogs on holistic health had the "Woodstock generation" look about them. Today the alternative health field has grown into a major industry that is gaining respect and acceptance.

Mainstream health organizations are incorporating holistic methods into their procedures at an ever increasing rate. In much the same way that New Age beliefs and techniques are creeping into business and education, so individuals who have become transformed are actively trying to bring these methods into their respective health fields. One New Age publication put it very well when they said, "The wholistic model derives its view of health from the same core values that animate other segments of New Age life."² The concept is that the path to true spiritual well-being is connecting with one's "higher wisdom" or "true inner being." You do not have to look into the holistic health movement very deeply to realize that the underlying elements are nothing more than the teachings of the Ancient Wisdom.

The holistic health field is multi-faceted. It incorporates much that is practical and useful. Nutrition, herbs, chiropractic, and massage are some of the practices found in holistic health that have no direct connection with New Age spirituality. Acupressure/acupuncture is more controversial. The subject matter for this chapter primarily concerns energy healing, crystal work, and meditation as stress reduction therapy; categories that could be classified as *transformational* in nature.

ENERGY HEALING

In the book, *Forever Fit*, Cher speaks of a friend of hers who is a metaphysical "healer":

> ...She heals with her hands and, boy, if she puts her hands on you, you *know* you've been touched. Even near your body you feel it. It's simply unbelievable...But she is truly tuned into some kind of higher power.³

Occultists believe that man has more than one body, that there are other invisible "bodies" superimposed on the physical body. They refer to one of these as the "etheric body" and believe there lies within it energy centers called "chakras" (pronounced shock-ra). The term chakra means "whirling wheel" in Sanskrit, the ancient Hindu language. They were seen by those with "clairvoyant" powers as spinning balls of psychic energy. It is taught that there are seven chakras which start at the base of the spine and end at the "crown chakra" at the top of the head.

Each chakra is supposed to have a different function corresponding to certain "levels of awareness." The chakras act as conduits or conductors for what is called *kundalini* or "serpent" energy. They say this force lies coiled, but dormant, at the base of the spine like a snake. When awakened during meditation, it is supposed to travel up the spine activating each chakra as it surges upward. When the kundalini force hits the crown chakra, the person experiences "enlightenment" or "Self-realization." This mystical current results in the person "knowing" himself to be "God." That is why kundalini is sometimes referred to as the "divine energy." Consider the following explanation:

> All the meditative techniques require power—energy in their performance. The more energy you can generate, the greater their performance. Actually, it is not physical energy that you use here, but psychic energy (called in India, prana) which you draw from the infinite universe. The reservoir of this energy in the human body is also known by a Hindu name—it is called 'kundalini.' The kundalini is looked upon

by Oriental mystics as being like a coiled
serpent; it is sometimes named "The
Serpent Power." In the East, the serpent is
not regarded as a symbol of evil, it is a
symbol of divinity.[4]

The *chakra system* is the basis for virtually all energy-
healing techniques. In energy-healing, the power is channeled into the patient, thus bringing about the desired
"wellness" and "wholeness" of the person receiving it.
Currently, there are a number of energy-healing systems.
Although they have different names, the energy that they
use is from the same source.

REIKI

One of the fastest growing New Age healing techniques being used today is *Reiki*, (pronounced ray-key), a
Japanese word which translates "universal life energy" or
"God energy." It has also been referred to as "the
Radiance Technique." Reiki is an ancient Tibetan healing
system which was "rediscovered" by a Japanese man in
the 1800's and has only recently been brought to the West.

The technique consists of placing the hands on the
recipient and then activating the energy to *flow through*
the practitioner into the recipient. One practitioner
described the experience in the following way.

When doing it, I become a channel
through which this force, this juice of the
universe, comes pouring from my palms
into the body of the person I am touching,

sometimes lightly, almost imperceptibly,
sometimes in famished sucking drafts. I
get it even as I'm giving it. It surrounds
the two of us, patient and practitioner.[5]

One obtains this power by being "attuned" by a Reiki
master. This is done in four sessions in which the master
activates the chakras, creating an open channel for the
energy. The attunement process is not made known for
general information, but is held in secrecy for only those
being initiated.

One of the main reasons Reiki has become so popular
is because it is apparently a pleasurable experience. Those
who have experienced Reiki report feeling a powerful
sense of warmth and security. One woman, now a Reiki
master, remarked after her first encounter: "I don't know
what this is you've got but I just have to have it."[6] People
don't make such comments unless there is an appeal
involved. A successful business woman gave Reiki the
following praise:

Reiki should be available through
every medical, chiropractic and mental
health facility in this country. Your fees
are a small price to pay for such impressive results. I don't know how Reiki
works, but it works; that's all that counts
in my book.[7]

They say that once one is attuned he or she can never
lose the power, it is for life. They claim that distance is
not even a barrier for the Reiki energy, for the channel
may engage in what is called *absentee healing*, in which
the energy is "sent" over long distances, even thousands

of miles.

One master related: "Just by having the name or an object of the person or perhaps even a picture in your hand, you can send Reiki to them to wherever they are in the world."[8]

Tens of thousands are practicing Reiki in the United States today. In many cases, these are people who treat or work with others on a therapeutic basis, such as health professionals, body workers, chiropractors and counselors. In 1985, it was estimated that five to ten thousand people were learning Reiki *each year*.[9] This rate has most likely accelerated as Reiki becomes more widespread. Reiki is also very popular in Europe. I was told, in Holland alone 4,000 people a *month* become channelers.

What Reiki is *really* about is using this power to transform others into New Age consciousness. As one Reiki leader stated:

> "...it also makes a level of spiritual transformation available to non-meditators, that is usually reserved for those with a meditative path."[10]

Statements like this reveal that Reiki is in line with all the other New Age transformation efforts. It changes the way people *perceive reality*. Most practitioners acknowledge the truth of this. A German Reiki channeler made this comment:

> ...It frequently happens that patients will come into contact with new ideas after a few Reiki treatments. Some will start doing yoga or autogenous training or

start to meditate or practice some other
kind of spiritual method...fundamental
changes will set in and new things will
start to develop. You will find it easier to
cast off old, outlived structures and you
will notice that you are being led and
guided more and more.[11]

I have a friend who works for a major bank. She discovered her name was on a list to receive massage treat-
ments from a man the bank had brought in for "stress
reduction." She found out he was to work with *every*
department at the corporate head office. When she told
me the man's name, I recalled the following.

Two years before, I had seen a booth at the State Fair
where this man and two others were giving massages. On
a hunch, I walked up and asked, "Does anyone here do
Reiki?" This man's head immediately popped up and he
replied with fervor, "I do, want a treatment?" I politely
declined and departed, much to his displeasure. Before I
left I picked up his brochure and made sure to remember
his name.

A while later, I saw his advertisement in a New Age
resource guide which said he specialized in "corporate
stress reduction."

What concerned me was that Reiki apparently can be
combined with regular massage technique without the
recipient knowing it. A letter in the Reiki Journal
revealed:

Reiki is a whole new experience when
used in my massage therapy practice.

Massage, I thought, would be an excellent
tool to spread the radiance of this universal energy and a client would benefit and
really *not realize what a wonderful
growth was happening in his or her
being* (italics mine).[12]

What this means is that one person (using Reiki
covertly) could transform an *entire corporation* without
anyone knowing what was taking place!

THERAPEUTIC TOUCH

Therapeutic touch is another widespread healing tech-
nique. This method was developed and promoted by Dr.
Delores Krieger, a professor of nursing at New York
University.

While Reiki is obtained by being attuned by a master,
Therapeutic touch is acquired by standard metaphysical
meditation commonly referred to as "centering." Teachers
of Therapeutic touch readily acknowledge that "centering
is probably the most important part of the entire process...."[13]

A practitioner related that when she first encountered
therapeutic touch in graduate nursing school, it was "the
craziest, kookiest stuff I'd ever seen or heard."[14] This
skepticism did not last. "I got through the semester,
though, and in the process Dr. Krieger performed the pro-
cedure on me. It was then I knew something very real was
going on, so I continued to learn about it, and practice
it."[15] Like the others, she attributes this power to "the individual Higher Self" and feels that this type of healing is

not just for the body, but also as being "very spiritual."[16]

CRYSTALS

Although it may appear to be a fad to the average person, the metaphysical use of quartz crystal, like most New Age practices, dates back to early history. It's usage is found in virtually all occult traditions. Today, crystals are being used by New Agers for basically two reasons—to enhance their meditation and to store "energy." They say that just having a crystal in their presence while they meditate deepens their level of consciousness and resulting experiences are more powerful.

Metaphysicians will tell you that the crystals by themselves contain no power or ability. They function as *amplifiers* for the energy during meditation. One of them related:

> An interesting phenomenon happens when you begin to work with crystals—for whatever reason. You will start becoming aware of an energy or force greater than what you presently contain. This force has been called your Higher Self, and it encompasses 'that which you are capable of becoming.' It is your perfected self. Quartz crystals, in their wonderfully helpful way, will help you tune into this higher aspect of yourself.[17]

These energies are then used by the crystal healer to bring about supposed physical, mental, and spiritual health in the patient. As with Reiki, Therapeutic Touch, and other energy healing techniques, crystal work is also based on the "chakra system." One practitioner revealed: "Crystal work, psychic work, healing work, or any work of a metaphysical nature, uses the higher chakras or energy centers; the third eye, crown, throat and/or heart center."[18]

HANDS OF LIGHT

In her highly acclaimed book, *Hands of Light*, healer Barbara Ann Brennan lays out the dynamics of such practices as Reiki and therapeutic touch.

On page 44 of her book, it shows a drawn color picture of a woman doing energy healing on another woman. On each side of the healer are two figures that fit the description of the "beings of light" spoken of in my first chapter. The picture reveals that the power is coming from the two "entities" whom Brennan describes as "the Guides."

Brennan explains that:

The healer must first open and align herself with the cosmic forces. This means not only just before the healing, but in her life in general.[19]

These "cosmic forces" also have names. Brennan tells of an exchange between her and a being who calls himself "Heyoan," who reveals to her: "Enlightenment is the goal; healing is a by-product."[20] What he meant by this is that the forces behind energy healing are really pushing the "man-is-God" view and any physical benefits are just the bait.

Anyone considering undergoing *any* "chakra-based" energy therapy should first seriously consider Brennan's sobering revelation that "I and Heyoan are one."[21]

STRESS MANAGEMENT

Stress is believed to be one of the leading causes of illness in America today. Millions of people suffer from disorders such as headaches, insomnia, nerves, and stomach problems because of excessive stress in their lives. In response to this situation, an army of practitioners have come forward to teach "relaxation skills" and "stress-reduction techniques" to the afflicted millions. A newspaper article proclaimed:

> Once a practice that appealed mostly to mystics and occult followers, meditation now is reaching the USA's mainstream....The medical establishment now recognizes the value of meditation and other mind-over-body states in dealing with stress-related illnesses.[22]

Does all meditation lead to New Age mysticism? Can a person meditate without having a metaphysical motive? Can it be done just to relax and get rid of tension without any *spiritual* side effects? These are legitimate questions. Suppose a company brings in a "stress specialist" to give a seminar and all employees are required to attend. What if a doctor prescribes meditation to relieve migraine

headaches? Say an aerobics instructor has the class lie on
their backs, close their eyes and do "breathing exercises."
Is there such a thing as "neutral" meditation?

I once asked John Klimo, who wrote what has been
called the definitive book on channeling, if the millions of
people who are meditating for stress reduction could
become transformed as a result. His response almost sent
me through the ceiling! "Most certainly," he replied with
marked enthusiasm. Being a channeler himself he viewed
the possibility of this with great expectation.

His optimism was well-founded. A comparison
between the meditation techniques used in stress reduction and the meditation used in New Age spirituality,
shows them to be basically the *same*. Both use either the
breathing or mantra method to still the mind. A blank
state of mind is all that is necessary for contact to occur.

Some well-known channelers became so because
meditation catapulted them into the world of spirit entities. Jach Pursel, who channels the immensely popular
"Lazaris," (see Chapter 2), explained how this "entity"
first came to him:

> Quite by surprise! I couldn't have pre-
> pared for it, that's for sure. It was 11 and
> 1/2 years ago, actually, October, 1974,
> and I was meditating....Then this voice
> started talking, she [his wife] grabbed a
> paper and pen and started writing as fast
> as she could. She had some awareness of
> metaphysics, had read about Edgar Cayce
> and others, so she wasn't totally unknow-
> ing to this whole area, but she certainly

didn't expect anything like this to happen
to me![23]

Kevin Ryerson, (featured in Shirley MacLaine's book
and television movie *Out On A Limb*), also got into channeling by accident. He joined a meditation group hoping
that he could tap into some "inner reservoir of creativity"
just as many in the business world are now doing. He
relates:

> When I entered this group, I had no
> intention or expectation of becoming a
> trance medium. But after six months, in
> the course of one of our sessions, I
> entered into a 'spontaneous channeling
> state,' as I refer to it now.[24]

John Randolph Price, founder of the Quartus
Foundation and instigator of the December 31 World
Healing Day Meditation, became involved in metaphysics
through this route. He revealed:

> Back when I was in the business
> world, the American Management
> Association put out a little book on medi-
> tation, which indicated that meditation
> was a way to attain peace of mind and
> reduce stress in a corporate environment.
> So I decided I'd try it....I learned that I
> could go into meditation as a human
> being, and within a matter of minutes,
> have transcended my sense of humanness.
> I discovered how to come into a new

sphere of consciousness. Consciousness actually *shifts*, and you move into a realm you may not have even known existed....[25]

So, can meditation be done without potential spiritual side effects? For those who still say no, give ear to the following:

> In alpha the mind opens up to nonordinary forms of communication, such as telepathy, clairvoyance, and precognition...In alpha the rational filters that process ordinary reality *are weakened or removed,* and the mind is *receptive to nonordinary realities* (italics mine).[26]

> *Almost without exception, those who channel effectively meditate regularly.* The process of channeling itself is an extension of the state of meditation...the best way to prepare, then, for channeling is by *meditation.*[27]

> ...The open door to Cosmic Consciousness is, of course, meditation.[28]

> First and foremost, almost all mediums agree on the significance and the importance of regular daily meditation. This single practice, above all others, is no doubt the very shaft that drives the wheel of development.[29]

Even though meditation can bring you seeming peace of mind and improved health I believe it is evident, by the accounts just given, that those who engage in it may find themselves in *similar* circumstances. According to New Ager Betty Bethards, "Meditation can, and does, change your life because it changes *you*."[30] Ken Wilber, another New Age writer and expert in the field of higher consciousness aptly put it: "If you're doing meditation correctly, you're in for some very rough and frightening times. Meditation as a 'relaxation response' is a joke."[31]

STEVEN HALPERN

Steven Halpern is widely regarded as the "father" of New Age music. His pieces have a spiritual aspect to them as well they should—many of them are channeled. Once, while meditating amongst the redwoods, he received "guidance" that there should be music that would "heal." What this "music" is intended to do is to literally induce a meditative state *just* by listening to it. When asked if this was possible he responded:

> There are ways of *stimulating alpha waves* — those brain waves that occur when a person is relaxed — by playing music that resonates with such harmonics. *These harmonics may be engineered right into compositions* — such as in my *Spectrum Suite* or *Crystal Suite* — which trigger the production of alpha waves.[32]

This is what the intention is. In the same interview, he revealed:

In regard to the field of New Age music, we recognize that it is music *specifically created* to help people *tune in to their Higher Nature* (italics mine).[33]

What is so significant about all this is that, he acknowledged: "...I've been able to get my music into many hospitals."[34] Consider this reality in light of his following revelation:

For me, a 'Gold Record' is when someone writes and tells me that a tape has touched their heart and opened them to a higher level of awareness and *attunement with their Higher Self* (italics mine).[35]

CHAPTER 6

New Age in Counseling and Self-Help

America is in sad shape. There are an estimated 18 million alcoholics in our country today with millions of others addicted to drugs. Another primary concern for many is weight control. Everyone knows how emotionally perilous romantic relationships can be. Noted columnist Ann Landers tells us that fifteen out of every twenty marriages are either unhappy or just mediocre.

To the New Age movement, these huge numbers of depressed and hurting people represent souls who need to get in touch with their "inner wisdom" to heal their troubled lives.

NEW AGE REHABILITATORS

The proponents of New Age techniques have permeated the fields of alcohol, drug, food addiction, and family therapy counseling. One publication referred to these "rehabilitators" as "pioneers on the forefront of the next stage of global and human development."[1]

The New Age program for America's addicted and distraught is remarkably simple in its approach. The idea is to replace substance and other abuses with "consciousness expansion." To change behavior such as drinking, snorting cocaine, popping pills, and mistreating each other, they get people into meditation.

One of the prime examples of this effort is the work of author, counselor, and theologian John Bradshaw. He has written three best-sellers: *Healing the Shame that Binds You, Bradshaw On: The Family* (which is also the name of his highly acclaimed series on PBS television), and *Homecoming.* His keen insights have made him the "bottom line" on family dysfunction. Talk-show host Oprah Winfrey informed her audience that "millions are lining up to hear his message." Newsweek stated that his seminars were being "sold out weeks in advance." Many have called him the leading evangelist of the recovery movement.

Bradshaw is a very articulate and effective speaker. His popularity springs from his ability to make sense of the root causes of personal and family dysfunction. He relates:

> Every addict has a god, be it work, money, booze, cocaine, a lover, a spouse, a child, gambling, nicotine, sex, food....No God ever had a more devoted follower. Addicts literally are ready and willing to give their life for their God.[2]

He explains that this is basically a "spiritual problem" that requires a *spiritual* remedy. For Bradshaw, that remedy is the Ancient Wisdom. He explains the meditation process the following way:

> *After much practice* you can create a state of mindlessness. This state is called the silence. Once the silence is created, an unused mental faculty is activated. It is a

form of intuition. With this faculty one can know God directly. Spiritual masters present a rather uniform witness on this point. They speak of this intuitive knowing variously as 'intuitive consciousness,' 'God consciousness,' or 'higher consciousness.' It is direct union with God....[3]

This "union" is with the classic occult concept of God. If God is everything and we are part of everything—then we are God. Bradshaw explains:

> "...*Each of us in his own way is the universe*. This is what all the great spiritual masters have been teaching us for centuries. The ego creates separation and illusion. Once beyond ego there is no separation. We are all one....[4]

To "know" yourself as you really are is a reference to the all-knowing "inner divinity" that New Agers seek to connect with. Bradshaw proclaims:

> The more we are truly ourselves, the more we are truly *Godlike*. To truly be ourselves, we need to accept our eternal mission and destiny. This consists in manifesting in a fully human way our Godlikeness. [5]

This is the message that "millions" are lining up to hear. He stated it very clearly on his December 2nd, 1990 PBS television special: "You (the audience) are a unique manifestation of the divine" and that "our greatest source of recovery and regeneration is higher consciousness" which he also referred to as "cosmic consciousness."

In addition he also acknowledged that he worked with "...this chakra energy."

It is not surprising, then, that Bradshaw has teamed up with Steven Halpern to put out a "transformative" cassette designed to help, "...those in recovery learn the ability to listen to their inner-selves and to *connect with the higher powers of our universe.*"[6]

Bradshaw has been a fan of Halpern for some time. He relates:

> I have been listening to Steven Halpern's music for over 12 years. It's helped me *meditate and center myself* which has made a tremendous difference in my life. His tapes continue to do wonders for me and the *thousands of people in my workshops* (italics mine).[7]

Melody Beattie is a popular author in the field of "co-dependency." She has written two top best-sellers, *Beyond Co-Dependency,* and *Co-Dependent No More* . Although these first two books were non-metaphysical she came out of the New Age closet with her third one, *Co-Dependents Guide to the Twelve Steps.*

In the chapter on "spiritual awakening" she says that to "connect with God" we need to open our minds to a "higher consciousness" and that we "build a connection to God by building a connection to *ourselves*" (italics mine).[8]

In the back of this book under "spiritual recovery book list," *fifteen* out of the sixteen books listed are hardcore New Age books including two that are channeled from a spirit guide.

The common theme of her comments in this section is that these books will "change," "alter," and "expand," one's concepts of God and spirituality, "breaking old patterns" and giving one a "new look at life."[9] Ironically the first book listed is "the Bible" which she calls "a favorite source" for those in recovery. Beattie had her own spiritual awakening not by reading the Bible but by smoking pot. While "high" one day in 1973, she experienced, "...the power of the Universe" speaking to her, and as a result, she now believes "that was my spiritual awakening. It transformed me. It transformed my life."[10]

Women Who Love Too Much by Robin Norwood, a family and child therapist, has sold over three million copies. My local public library purchased *nineteen* copies of this book to keep up with the demand.

The book deals with relationship addiction, or as Norwood explains, when your partner is inappropriate, uncaring or unavailable and yet you cannot give him up. Norwood's analysis of the problem hits home. She says that women should stop seeing men (especially those who are messed up) as the main source of their happiness and fulfillment. Norwood strongly emphasizes that women should not focus their happiness and well-being on human partners but rather on *spiritual* things. She explains why "spiritual development" is important:

> Without spiritual development, it is
> nearly impossible to let go of managing
> and controlling and to believe that all will
> work out as it is meant to....Without spiri-

tual development, it is nearly impossible
to let go of self-will, and without letting
go of self-will you will not be able to take
the next step.[11]

In the back of her book under Suggested Reading,
Norwood shows the *nature* of "the next step" very clearly.
She refers to Catherine Ponders' classic, *The Dynamic
Laws of Prosperity*, as "one of my favorite books on
metaphysics." The next book on the list is *The Game of
Life and How to Play It* by Florence Scovell Shinn. She
refers to it as a "masterpiece on metaphysics," and tells
her readers, "If you don't have a spiritual practice and
wish you did, this book may be a good place to start."[12]
  Norwood's second book, *Letters From Women Who
Love Too Much*, continues to point her readers in the New
Age direction. In turning to the Recommended Reading
list at the back of the book we see what titles she finds
herself "constantly recommending" to "those who are
already well on their way to recovery." One of these,
Lessons in Truth, by H. Emilie Cady, has been considered
by many to be a basic textbook of New Age teaching.
Another one, *Practicing the Presence*, by Joel Goldsmith,
teaches the same metaphysical program. His beliefs are
made clear by the following statement taken from that
book: "God is not found up in heaven....God is to be
found within us....It is within us that the contact must be
made...."[13] Norwood says, "This book [*Practicing the
Presence*] is the next step in training one's consciousness.
I also recommend any other book by Joel Goldsmith."[14]
  In addition to Bradshaw, Beattie, and Norwood, there
are a number of other writer/therapists who are directing

the scope of counseling toward the Ancient Wisdom. These include Charles L. Whitfield, M.D., *Healing the Child Within*; Ruth Fishel, *The Journey Within*; Wayne Kritsberg, *Gifts for Personal Growth & Recovery*; Patty McConnell, *A Workbook for Healing Adult Children of Alcoholics*; Julie Bowden and Herbert Gravitz, *Genesis: Spirituality in Recovery*; Philip Oliver-Diaz and Patricia O'Gorman, *12 Steps to Self-Parenting*; and Brenda Schaeffer, *Is It Love or Is It Addiction?*

Some others are Dorothy Corkille Briggs, Susan Jeffers, Ken Keyes, Gerald Jamplosky, Ellen Ratner, Sondra Ray, Vernon Howard, Louise L. Hay, Joy Miller, and Joan Borysenko.

This activity is also extensive at the local level. One woman's brochure claims she has trained "hundreds" of teachers, counselors, and addictions therapists in "the path of recovery and transformation" based on "ancient processes of self-awareness and empowerment."

I have also noticed an explosion of counseling centers in my local area that are metaphysically based, one of which boasts *ten therapists.*

FROM PHOBIA TO TRANSFORMATION

Human resource developer Robert Handly and writer Pauline Neff (author of *Tough Love*) have developed a program for helping people who suffer from anxiety and panic attacks. Handly, who was himself afflicted with this disorder, describes the method he used to successfully combat his problem:

> Whenever I went into alpha [meditation], I would feel a loving force within me, which made it possible for me to change. Gradually I began to realize that everyone else had this same universal, loving spirit. I resolved to deepen this knowledge of my spiritual self further through meditation. Eventually this goal was the one that melded all my goals into one. It made it truly possible for me to remain free of anxiety under all circumstances.[15]

Handly went on to create a popular self-help course based on this principle. As you have read, he does this through meditation, which he (and many others in the human potential/stress reduction field) refer to as the "alpha state." He relates the story of one man who conquered his eating disorder through use of this technique:

> Daily he sat and basked in this presence. And then a strange thing happened. When he passed by the refrigerator one night, his hand reached out to start to open the door. But as it did so, a calm but persistent force seemed to stop it in midair...'I lost weight because my spiritual self helped me,' Lane told me later. 'It also helped me overcome my anxiety. Somehow my spiritual self just took over, even though I never knew I had such a power within me.'[16]

Making this connection is the theme of Handly's whole program which he makes quite clear in this statement: "Although the other goals enabled me to overcome my phobia in tangible ways, the spiritual eventually led to a transformation experience. The real goal should be to make contact with this inner spirit and let it make wonderful changes in you."[17]

SELF-HELP TAPES

Self-help audio cassette tapes have recently become very popular. Through the use of hypnosis, they claim to change unwanted behavior by reprogramming the subconscious mind with subliminal messages that will influence the person toward the desired effect. These messages are appealing because they promise to resolve bad habits and develop good ones without pain or effort. This is supposedly accomplished by listening to the sounds of the ocean or soft music while the real message is being slipped to you subliminally (below your conscious awareness level).

The mind boggles at the array of promised benefits listed within audio cassette catalogs. Virtually every problem one could ever imagine is there, from acne to jet lag. The major themes in these tapes include success, overcoming phobias, health and fitness, erasing bad habits, sports, love and relationships. According to their catalogs, these tapes have helped thousands with backaches, stress, smoking, weight problems, and more. Although they come across as being strictly non-religious and purely scientific, many of these programs are clearly part of the human potential aspect of the New Age movement. You do not have to look very hard to find the Ancient Wisdom mixed in.

The Gateways Institute actively promotes using these tapes. Their sixty-minute TV film, *Mind Power*, is narrated by the founder of the company, Jonathan Parker. The viewer may not have an inkling that there is a spiritual aspect to what Mr. Parker is promoting, but one look at the company's catalog shows quite the contrary. The introduction begins: "Welcome! Join us as we explore the illuminating world of self-transformation and higher consciousness."

Jonathan Parker is described as having a "scholarly background" in such things as "transpersonal [metaphysical] psychology and higher consciousness studies."[18]

Even though most of the tapes deal with such topics as "coping with emotions" or the ever present "stress reduction," there are titles that reveal the metaphysical belief system behind this company. *Pathways To Mastership* (a twelve-tape set) is directed toward those who are "serious about self-development and spiritual progress." All twelve tapes deal with meditation, psychic unfoldment, mastery of the Higher Self, releasing the Kundalini energy, and the path to "God realization."[19]

In browsing further through the catalog, one finds such subjects as "balancing karma," Jonathan Parker allowing the "Master within" to speak through him, "encounters with interdimensional friends," "Trance Channeling...of wisdom from higher spiritual dimensions...what do non-physical entities do and what is their dimension like?"[20] All of this is clearly *hardcore* metaphysics.

Another popular self-help audio cassette company is

Potentials Unlimited. This company features racks of its tapes in many book, food, and variety stores for every conceivable problem. If this company offered only self-help, there would be no need to include them in this chapter. However, the catalog descriptions of some of their tapes would be hard to explain as being purely self-help. Consider the following description.

> THE AWAKENING #1
> The world is pregnant with anticipation. Some are expecting a messiah, others a second coming and still others, earth changes. All positions are correct and somewhat limited in their view. The message on this tape reveals a plan of unity and interdependence. A plan that requires you in order to complete itself, because you have the power to change the world when you awaken.[21]

The nature of this "plan that requires you in order to complete itself" is seen under the title *Chakra Meditation* in which you "unleash incredible cosmic and psychic powers" that "will benefit all mankind" when your chakras are energized.[22] This is what was meant by "when you awaken" in *The Awakening* tape. On the same page under *World Peace* it suggests that you "bring two or three people together and form a triangle of energy" to return the planet to "love, light, and life."[23] These three tapes plus five others of a similar context are listed under the title "Meditation Series."

The wife of the founder of Potentials Unlimited is

also the publisher of a magazine called *Connecting Link,* which is devoted entirely to spirit guide channeling. Interest in self-help tapes has given the purveyors of New Age transformation a great opportunity to spread their message to the masses. One such company stated:

> As the new age of peace and light begins, people are rediscovering their metaphysical awareness. They are learning how to manifest the reality they desire. Many are finding that audio self-help tapes can be a cosmic key that helps them unlock their own inner power.[24]

HYPNOSIS PRACTITIONERS

Practically every practitioner of hypnosis I have come across during my years of research has had a noticeable bent toward metaphysics. Even if it seems unapparent at first, many hypnotherapists engage in such therapies as "past life" regressions, which means that they accept reincarnation as being legitimate. Concerning this link, consider the following case recounted by a young woman:

> In 1978, I met a woman who was studying for her Ph.D. in psychology and experimenting with past life regression. I volunteered to be one of her subjects, and it was a day that has forever changed my life. During the regression, a 'consciousness,' which explained itself as a guide, began talking through me to the psycholo-

gist. I had the bizarre sensation of being
somewhere else, though at the time I was
vaguely conscious of a conversation taking place. I decided it was the most peculiar experience. My first experience as a
medium![25]

Another woman recalled:

One of my earliest and most powerful
hypnotherapy experiences was meeting
my inner guide.[26]

Now a hypnotherapist herself, she is doing the same
thing for those who come to her for a variety of problems.
She states:

Although meeting my inner guide was
a very moving experience, I also have the
great fortune of helping others meet their
guides.[27]

Although it would be ridiculous to suggest that everyone who gets hypnotized automatically winds up as a
channeler, these incidents would explain why so many
hypnotherapists *are* also involved with the Ancient
Wisdom. I believe there is a link between the hypnotic
state and the meditative state. This relationship between
hypnotherapy and New Age beliefs brings to mind the old
adage "where there's smoke there's fire."

SEEDBEARERS

Earlier, we saw that metaphysics can be taught as *either religion or science.* I believe this chapter illustrates that point well.

By calling itself transpersonal [beyond the ego] psychology, this New Age spearhead is being enthusiastically incorporated into therapy settings around the world. At the 11th International Transpersonal conference in September 1990, which featured John Bradshaw as the main speaker, hundreds of "therapists" came together to plan new strategies to make this an even more widespread mode of treatment.

I firmly believe that all of these therapists are sincere, caring people with a desire to help others. They feel they have uncovered the true remedy for what plagues the human condition. It "worked" for them, they have seen it "work" for others, and they want to share this seemingly wonderful discovery with as many as they can reach.

Keep in mind that there are thousands of counselors and therapists who are no different than those described in this chapter. They are having an *enormous* impact on literally *millions* of people. Their collective goal is to replace "co-dependency" with transformation. As New Age therapist Jacquelyn Small exhorts: "Those of you who carry the Transformer consciousness need to remember: You are standing right at the entrance of the new era—and you are its Seedbearer."[28]

CHAPTER 7

New Age in Religion

One of the main reasons many Christian pastors fail to take the New Age movement seriously is that they are not adept at effectively measuring its real strength. They are accustomed to assessing the prestige and influence of a spiritual movement by its number of churches, attendance records, or television and radio programs. Since they do not see New Age churches on every corner, they tend to discount any cause for alarm. The following information may be of interest to those who are skeptical.

Just as business, health care, education, counseling, and other areas of society are being influenced by those who have had transformation experiences, so is *American religion*. This influence is becoming so widespread it now appears that mainstream religions are playing a prominent role in spreading New Age consciousness. Many people would be quite surprised to find that meditation has made its way into both Catholic and Protestant churches on a large scale. Although some would argue that it is not New Age meditation but rather a form of "prayer," I would beg to differ.

Upon close examination, the methods used (mantra, breathing) are *identical* to New Age techniques. Only the connotation is changed. Countless times I have come across such terms as "holistic spirituality" or "combining the mystical traditions of both East and West." Frequently, the Hindu or Buddhist source of these "spiritual exercises" will be proclaimed openly.

CENTERING PRAYER

In the book, *Finding Grace at the Center*, which was written by several proponents of centering prayer, the following statements are made:

> We should not hesitate to take the fruit of the age-old wisdom of the East and 'capture' it for Christ. Indeed, those of us who are in ministry should make the necessary effort to acquaint ourselves with as many of these Eastern techniques as possible....Many Christians who take their prayer life seriously have been greatly helped by Yoga, Zen, TM, and similar practices, especially where they have been initiated by reliable teachers and have a solidly developed Christian faith to give inner form and meaning to the resulting experiences.[1]

In view of this, it is no wonder that I encountered a woman in a Christian bookstore who enthusiastically told me that in her church "we use a *mantra* to get in touch with God."

Being touted as an "ancient prayer form" the "centering prayer" employs a mantra (called the "prayer word") that allows one to empty the mind by chanting "Jesus," "God" or "love" rather than "om" or "Krishna."

Centering prayer groups are flourishing in mainstream religious bodies today. Many times those who embrace these practices are the most active and creative people in the congregation. They are seen by many as bringing a new vitality to the church.

One widely popular book on this is *Sadhana: A Way To God* by Anthony de Mello, S.J. Sadhana, according to de Mello, means "spiritual path." This book is very open in its acknowledgement of Eastern mysticism as an enrichment to Christian spirituality. De Mello lets his readers know at the very beginning just where he is coming from:

> A Jesuit friend once told me that he approached a Hindu guru for initiation in the art of prayer. The guru said to him, *"Concentrate on your breathing."* My friend proceeded to do just that for about five minutes. Then the guru said, '*The air you breathe is God. You are breathing God in and out. Become aware of that, and stay with that awareness.*'[2]

The following statement by de Mello could have been made by *any* New Ager:

> ...I want you now to discover the revelation that silence brings...[3]

Silence, of course, is the "blank" mind that you have been reading about. This word is used as a buzz word by many in metaphysics. When a person is in this state, they are "open" to the "Universe."

De Mello explains what it is like to experience "silence," which is the logical progression in the *Sadhana* process—the altered state of consciousness.

There will be moments when the stillness of the *blank* will be so powerful that
it will make all exercise and all effort on
your part impossible. In such moments it
is no longer you who goes in quest of
stillness. It is stillness that *takes possession of you* and overwhelms you. When
this happens, you may safely, and prof-
itably, let go of all effort (which has
become impossible, anyway) and surren-
der to this overpowering stillness within
you (italics mine).[4]

Sadhana has had an enormous impact on both clergy
and laity. One source revealed:

This book has come to be recognized
universally as a *masterpiece* in the art of
teaching people *how to pray*. After its first
publication in 1979, it ranked among the
top U.S. Catholic best sellers for many
years. Just to read it is a captivating and
challenging experience. More than 20
translations have been published. Now all
over the world this classic text has been
acclaimed as the best how-to-do-it book
on prayer available in any language.[5]

It is often used as a textbook to teach people how to
"pray." Catholic parishes, nursing facilities, hospitals,
retirement centers, and religious communities are using it
on a regular basis.[6] It has been highly praised by church

leaders and theologians. The back cover of the book includes the following statement made by a leading church figure: "This book...is perhaps the best book available today in English for Christians on how to pray, meditate, and contemplate."[7]

I'm sure many of these people would be surprised if they learned what the Hindu connotation of *Sadhana* meant. A dictionary on Hinduism reveals the following:

> Siddhis [psychic powers] are also considered to be the direct or indirect result of a quest for enlightenment or knowledge. The pursuit of any method for attaining to such knowledge is termed *sadhana*, 'gaining;' the person practicing sadhana is called a *sadhaka* (fem. *sadhika*), and the successful sadhaka is a *sadhu*. Since siddhis are magical in character, the terms *sadhana* and *sadhu* are also frequently used for sorcery and sorcerer respectively.[8]

The literal meaning for *Sadhana: A Way to God*, according to this definition, would then be "*Sorcery: A Way to God!*"

Meditation is also being taught within the parochial school systems, generally at the high school and college levels. Students at Catholic schools have revealed to me that mantra meditation is part of their curriculum and that these classes are lead by priests. One Catholic high school textbook entitled *Your Faith and You: A Synthesis of Catholic Belief* revealed the following in the chapter entitled "Prayer, Seeking Union With God:"

> Numerous Catholic retreat houses
> offer 'Yoga retreats' or teach Zen medita-
> tion methods. But these techniques are
> totally removed from the Buddhist or
> Hindu faiths. They are often used by
> Christians to help them develop a con-
> scious faith relationship with Christ in
> prayer. Likewise, the Buddhist or Hindu
> uses these same techniques to enter into a
> deeper union with God as his own reli-
> gion has taught him to believe in him.[9]

I wonder how it is possible that Christians can use the
"same techniques" that Buddhists and Hindus use to reach
their gods without, in fact, *reaching their gods*.

Metaphysical meditation remains exactly the same no
matter what name you tag it with. Changing the mantras
does not make it "Christian."

What is happening is that this melding of meditative
practices is producing some major changes in
Christendom. Many are being taught that centering prayer
is the most direct route to God. This in turn, is producing
what one writer termed "full Christianity." He explained:

> Indeed today Catholics practice Zen
> meditation. There are Christian-Hindu
> monasteries in India. And Fr. Raimundo
> Panikkar has suggested that Indian philos-
> ophy might prove a better base for
> Christian theology than Aristotle. Thomas

Merton predicted that the 21st century would belong to two things: Christianity and Zen. Today these great traditions as well as others are meeting one another in a spirit of humble inquiry. Perhaps it is just this coming together of our world traditions that will provide the spiritual impetus needed to usher in a new age of the Spirit.[10]

FILLING THE VACUUM

Why are the mainstream denominations so open to meditative and holistic practices? David R. Griffen, professor of theology at a United Methodist college in Clairmont, California, stated: "A spiritual vacuum exists in organized religion that might be filled by theologies that draw—for better or worse—from what is called parapsychology, paranormal studies, psychic phenomena and, somewhat pejoratively, the 'New Age' movement."[11]

New Agers have become very much aware of this "spiritual vacuum" and have directed their efforts toward filling it. Metaphysical leader James Fadiman made the following observation:

The traditional religious world is just beginning to make changes, but it's a slow process—denomination by denomination. When religious institutions begin to lose members year after year, they eventually become aware that they're not meeting peoples needs. Before long they're scurrying around looking for innovative programs and improvements.[12]

Even atheists have observed this trend. Science-fiction writer Richard E. Geis commented in his personal journal that:

> The mainstream Christians are lip-service religions in the main, convenience religions, social religions, and they are the ones most subject to erosion and defections and infiltration and subversion. A large and successful effort seems to have been made by the 'occultists' New Age planners to dilute and alter the message of most of the mainstream Christian religions.[13]

This is made evident by a quote which appeared in a newspaper interview with the owner of a New Age bookstore. She revealed:

> A lot of people come in who are very Christian. They are looking, by whatever means, to move closer to God on an individual basis."[14]

This shows that a great number of people who consider themselves to be Christians have a rather dull and dreary attitude toward their faith. They are looking for something to fill the void.

CHRISTIAN TOLERANCE

The following is a good barometer of Christian tolerance to New Age ideas. Psychologist M. Scott Peck has written a phenomenal best seller on psychology and spiritual growth entitled *The Road Less Traveled*. The book contains many useful insights and suggestions for dealing with life's problems, which is why it has generated the interest it has. But the book also incorporates the central theme of the Ancient Wisdom:

> God wants us to become himself (or Herself or Itself). We are growing toward godhood. God is the goal of evolution. It is God who is the source of the evolutionary force and God who is the destination. This is what we mean when we say that He is the Alpha and the Omega, the beginning and the end.
>
> ...It is one thing to believe in a nice old God who will take good care of us from a lofty position which we ourselves could never begin to attain. It is quite another to believe in a God who has it in mind for us precisely that we should attain His position, His power, His wisdom, His identity.[15]

Madame Blavatsky and Alice Bailey could not have said it any better. Peck reveals where he is coming from when he says, "But (*The Road*) is a sound New Age book, not a flaky one."[16] This book, which has been on the New

York Times best seller list for over 400 weeks, has been incredibly popular in Christian circles for years. Peck himself says, "The book sells best in the Bible Belt."[17] By viewing the continuing influence of Peck in American religious circles, one would find the following significant: Peck has enthusiastically endorsed some blatantly New Age books, *Living in Love With Yourself* by Barry A. Ellsworth, and *The Coming of the Cosmic Christ* by Matthew Fox. Of the former, an account of a man getting in touch with his Higher Self and seeing "god in everyone," he says: "The book's vulnerability is both touching and beautiful...a book to be closely read."[18] Of the latter, which echoes the New Age "mystical" theme, he states: "Fox's most daring pioneering work yet, stimulating us to the kind of resurrection of values and practice *required for planetary salvation"* (italics mine).[19]

The source of Peck's spiritual paradigm can be seen in the following information taken from a magazine article about him: "Peck himself moved gradually from an interest in *Eastern* mystical religions toward *Christian* mysticism" (italics mine).[20]

Another example is a spiritual resource and retreat center that advertised, "Discover the healing power within you." This center promoted such things as Zen, yoga, Reiki, and self-hypnosis for "spiritual growth." What astounded me, though, was the endorsements from a number of Protestant religious leaders on the back of their brochure. One senior pastor recommended it for "inner growth and renewal." Another one, who was a counselor at a pastoral care center, stated that it "encourages people to embrace wholeness." Most surprising, the president of a large denominational college "highly recommended" the leadership of this institute.[21]

A GLOBAL RELIGION

What is happening to mainstream Christianity is the same thing that is happening to business, health, education, counseling, and other areas of society. Christendom is being cultivated for a role in the New Age. The entity, Raphael, explains this very clearly in the *Starseed Transmissions:*

> We work with all who are vibrational-
> ly sympathetic; simple and sincere people
> who feel our spirit moving, but for the
> most part, *only within the context of their
> current belief system* (italics mine).[22]

He is saying that they "work," or interact, with people who open their minds to them in a way that fits in with the person's *current beliefs.* In the context of Christianity this means that those meditating will think that they have contacted "God," when in reality they have connected up with Raphael's kind (who are more than willing to impersonate whomever the person wishes to reach so long as they can link with them).

This ultimately points to a global religion based on meditation and mystical experience. New Age writer David Spangler explained it the following way:

> There will be several religious and
> spiritual disciplines as there are today,
> each serving different sensibilities and

affinities, each enriched by and enriching
the particular cultural soil in which it is
rooted. However, there will also be a
planetary spirituality. There will be a
more widespread understanding and experience of the holistic nature of reality,
resulting in a shared outlook that today
would be called mystical. Mysticism has
always overflowed the bounds of particular religious traditions, and in the new
world this would be even more true.[23]

The rise of centering prayer is causing many churches
to become *agents of transformation.* Those who practice
it tend to embrace this one-world-religion idea. One of
the main proponents of centering prayer had this revelation:

It is my sense, from having meditated
with persons from many different [non-
Christian] traditions, that *in the silence
we experience a deep unity.* When we go
beyond the portals of the rational mind
into *the experience,* there is only one God
to be experienced....I think it has been the
common experience of all persons of
good will that when we sit together
Centering we experience *a solidarity* that
seems to *cut through all our philosophi-
cal and theological differences* (italics
mine).[24]

Religion, therefore, would be like a dairy herd. Each
cow may look different on the outside, but the milk would

all be the *same*. The different religious groups would maintain their own separate identities, but a universal spiritual practice would bind them together. Not so much a one-world church as a one-world spirituality.

Catholic writer Mathew Fox has called this "deep ecumenism." He believes that all world religions will eventually be bound together by the "cosmic Christ" principle, which is another term for the Higher Self.

As incredible as this may sound, it appears to be happening now.

CHAPTER 8

Why is the New Age Wrong?

In the first seven chapters of this book, we examined the origin, essence, and thrust of metaphysics today. I do not agree with the view that the New Age is the path to the Golden Age of global peace and harmony.

But after seven years of research, I fully understand why so many people *have* embraced metaphysics and why they seek transformation for humanity as a whole. By and large, they have rejected orthodox (old paradigm) Christianity as being unacceptable, but still want to retain spiritual meaning and a utopian vision in their lives. In addition, they see metaphysics as helpful towards improving the quality of their daily lives, whether it be better health, more loving relationships, inner peace, or guidance for success and prosperity. They would think it the height of ignorance and folly to condemn such seemingly wonderful ways to better the human condition.

Many would reject a challenge of New Age consciousness from a Christian viewpoint as being the result of misinformation. It is widely believed in New Age circles that Jesus Christ was Himself a metaphysician of great stature. They quote verses where Jesus proclaims, "The kingdom of God is within you" (which they claim is talking about the Higher Self), "Be still and know that I am God" (which they claim is a reference to meditation), and "Greater things shall ye do than I," meaning New

Agers can have his "powers." As far out as this may sound to many Christian readers, New Age adherents are quite sincere in this belief. They firmly argue that reincarnation was originally in the Bible but was taken out at the Council of Nicea so that church and state could better control the common people by fear. Although there are still plenty of skeptics and critics, these beliefs are becoming less offensive and more acceptable all the time.

One of the most common New Age attitudes is that there are *many* paths to God and that it is wrong to judge or condemn another person's path because not all people are suited for the same one. They argue that each one should find the path best for them.

TO JUDGE OR NOT TO JUDGE

There are two questions to be answered here:

1. Is it right to judge?
2. Do all paths lead to God?

Jesus Christ foretold in Matthew 7:22-23:

> Many will say to me in that day, 'Lord, Lord, have we not prophesied in thy name? and in thy name have cast out devils? and in thy name done many wonderful works?' And then will I profess unto them, 'I never knew you: depart from me, ye that work iniquity.'

I find it most interesting that people who were doing "many wonderful works" or miraculous works in *His* name were, in reality, working "iniquity" or evil. This leads me to believe that there is great deception occuring.

The verses also tell me that all paths *do not* lead to God and, because they do not, one had better judge which path *is* correct. Many people, of course, counter with, "Judge not, that ye be not judged." However, taken in context, this verse (Matthew 7:1), is talking about hypocrisy in human behavior and not about withholding critical examination of spiritual teachings. Galatians 1:8-9 bears out the necessity to *evaluate* spiritual teaching with proper discernment. Paul warns:

> But though we, or an angel from heaven, *preach any other gospel unto you than that which we have preached unto you, let him be accursed* (italics mine).

And 2 John 1:9-11 says:

> Whosoever transgresseth, and abideth not in the doctrine of Christ, *hath not God.* He that abideth in the *doctrine* of Christ, he *hath both the Father and the Son.* If there come any unto you, and bring not this doctrine, receive him not into your house, neither bid him God speed: For he that biddeth him God speed is partaker of his evil deeds (italics mine).

And again in Ephesians 5:11, "...have no fellowship with the unfruitful works of darkness, but rather *reprove them*" (italics mine).

How may we reprove something if we don't deter-

mine whether or not it fits the bill of "unfruitful works?"
Second Timothy 3:16-17 says:

> All scripture is given by inspiration of
> God, and is profitable for doctrine, *for
> reproof, for correction,* for instruction in
> righteousness: That the man of God may
> be perfect [complete], thoroughly fur-
> nished [fully equipped] unto all good
> works (italics mine).

FAMILIAR SPIRITS

Noticing the New Age propensity for also quoting
Bible verses to support the claims of metaphysics, I have
focused on the obvious *conflict* between the Ancient
Wisdom and the God of the Bible that runs from Genesis
through Revelation. The continuity of this apparent contrast is undeniable to the point that any New Ager would
have to acknowledge that it exists. This is the only foundation for any logical Christian opposition to metaphysics. Notice the list of metaphysical arts in
Deuteronomy 18:9-12:

> When thou art come into the land
> which the Lord thy God giveth thee, thou
> shalt not learn to do after the *abomina-
> tions of those nations.* There shall not be
> found among you any one that maketh his
> son or his daughter to pass through the
> fire, or that useth divination [a psychic],
> or an observer of times [festivals connect-
> ed to nature worship], or an enchanter

[one who manipulates people by occult power], or a witch [woman who uses occult power]. Or a charmer [hypnotist], or a *consulter with familiar spirits* [one who receives advice or knowledge from a spirit], or a wizard [one who uses a spirit to do his will], or a necromancer [one who believes he is contacting the dead]. For all that do these things are an abomination unto the Lord: and because of these abominations the Lord thy God doth drive them out from before thee (italics mine).

The word abomination in verse 12 means "abhorrent" or "disgusting." Please note the reference to *familiar spirits* in the following verses from Leviticus. This term is found throughout the Old Testament and has a negative connotation. "And the soul that turneth after such as have *familiar spirits,* and after wizards, to go a whoring after them, I will even set my face against that soul, and will cut him off from among his people" (Leviticus 20:6, italics mine).

Creative Visualization by Shakti Gawain, which could be called one of the bibles of the New Age movement (over two million copies have been sold), explains the basic process. First comes "relaxing into a deep, quiet meditative state of mind," which is to be done every morning and afternoon. This opens the "channel" for "higher wisdom and guidance to come to you." Gawain then describes the nature of this "guidance":

The inner guide is known by many different names, such as your counselor, spirit guide, imaginary friend, or master. It is a higher part of yourself, which can come to you in many different forms, but usually comes in the form of a person or being whom you can talk to and relate to as a wise and loving friend....Your guide is there for you to call on anytime you need or want extra guidance, wisdom, knowledge, support, creative inspiration, love or companionship. Many people who have established a relationship with their guide meet them everyday in their meditation.[1]

What Shakti Gawain is talking about is the same thing spoken of in Deuteronomy 18—*familiar spirits*. The so-called "Higher Self" is nothing more than a familiar spirit out to manipulate those people who open themselves to it. It has been common in Christian circles to speak of them as demons. The word demon comes from the Greek term *deamonion*, which literally means "spirit guide." Familiar spirits make contact while the person's mind is in neutral, try to establish a strong connection, and the result is the control of the person by the spirit. As one book says, "Your Higher Self must be placed in a position where it will hold dominion over all areas of your being."[2]

That is why in Ephesians 6:12, the apostle Paul warns us that "we wrestle not against *flesh and blood*, but against principalities, against powers, against the rulers of the darkness of this world, against spiritual wickedness in high places" (italics mine).

He is saying that there are non-human powers (forces) that are in opposition to God. The nature of this is apparent to anyone who takes a close look at metaphysics with this verse in mind. At a certain point, influence and guidance from the familiar spirit progresses to outright possession. This, I believe, is what the kundalini effect is. One New Ager explained it the following way:

> Before, kundalini had seemed like a fable to me, fascinating and appealing, but as improbable in its way as God talking to Moses through a burning bush or Jesus raising the dead. But now I was sometimes aware, toward the end of the third stage of Dynamic Meditation, of something moving as elusively as neon up my spine, flashing like lightning in my limbs. When, in the fifth and final stage, I danced, I now sensed myself moved by a force more powerful, more inventive, than any I could consciously summon.[3]

I believe that Raphael and Alice Bailey's "Tibetan" are familiar spirits. I also believe they are revealing their "plan of operation" in their writings. The intent of these beings can be seen by what the following metaphysical practitioners convey:

> What really occurs is that you draw upon the God-qualities that live within you, and you are One with Cosmic Truth. *No longer will God be something that exists outside of yourself* (italics mine).[4]

>...It is not necessary to 'have faith' in any power outside of yourself.[5]

THE ANGEL OF LIGHT

Who do you think would want you to believe something like that? Who would want you to believe that God does not exist *outside of yourself*—that you don't need to have faith in anything "external." New Age writer/philosopher David Spangler reveals *who* in his book *Reflections on the Christ* when he writes:

>Some being has to take these energies into his consciousness and substance and channel them as it were to those other beings who must receive them, in this case humanity. The being who chose to embody these energies and to be in essence the angel of man's inner evolution is the being we know as Lucifer.[6]

He lays out the entire program behind the New Age movement in the following explanation:

>He [Lucifer] comes to make us aware of our power within, to draw to ourselves experience. He comes to make us aware of the power of creative manifestation which we wield. When you are working with the laws of manifestation you are in essence manifesting a Luciferic principle....[7]

Even if Spangler had not written these words, the link between Lucifer and the New Age movement would still be evident to Christians from reading 2 Corinthians 11:13-15:

> For such are false apostles, deceitful workers, transforming themselves into the apostles of Christ. And no marvel; for *Satan himself is transformed into an angel of light.* Therefore it is no great thing if his ministers also be transformed as the *ministers of righteousness*; whose end shall be according to their works (italics mine).

For this deception to be effective, he would have to come as an "angel of light." To judge a belief system as being satanic, one should compare how close it comes to Satan's own statements about himself. God is asking him, "How art thou fallen from heaven, O Lucifer, son of the morning! How art thou cut down to the ground, which didst weaken the nations!" (Isa. 14:12). Then He reminds Satan of his own words when he challenged God:

> For thou [Satan] hast said in thine heart, 'I will ascend into heaven, I will exalt my throne above the stars of God: I will sit also upon the mount of the congregation, in the sides of the north: I will ascend above the heights of the clouds; *I will be like the most High'* (Isaiah 14:13-14, emphasis added).

Then later, when Satan deceived Eve in the Garden, he said, "For God doth know that in the day ye eat thereof, then your eyes shall be opened, and *ye shall be as gods*, knowing good and evil" (Genesis 3:5, italics mine). Without a doubt, the New Age movement *fits that bill.*

THE "WILES" OF SATAN

In Ephesians 6:11, it warns: "Put on the whole armour of God, that ye may be able to stand against the *wiles* of the devil" (italics mine).

The word *wiles* in this verse translates "ingenious trap" or "snare." In order for a trap to be effective, proper bait is needed—something that is alluring, that looks and feels valid. For example, let's take the case of Reiki. The average Reiki practitioner would think it outrageous and ridiculous that someone would even *suggest* that Reiki was linked to Satan. One Reiki master offered this comment on the positive nature of Reiki:

> During Reiki treatments, people sometimes note warmth, tingling, deep relaxation, a release of mental or emotional stress, a feeling of detachment from cares and worries, and release from pain, soreness, stiffness, swelling, etc. Most people describe a general feeling of well-being and of having felt nurtured and touched by unconditional healing love.[8]

Does this sound like something that is satanic? Most people would not only say no but feel that something of this nature probably would have to come from God.

In *The Reiki Factor*, Reiki master Barbara Ray says, "In addition, Reiki is for maintaining health and balance as well as for attaining higher consciousness, spiritual growth, and ultimately, enlightenment."[9]

Enlightenment is the same as Self-realization, especially in the context of a metaphysical practice. When a Christian hears someone claim to be "God" he immediately recognizes the pronouncements of Satan, "Ye shall be as gods," and "I shall be like the most High."

In view of this, the only logical conclusion is that the power behind Reiki is *satanic*. The key is not to think in terms of how the popular culture sees Satan, but rather how the writers of the Bible saw Satan—a master deceiver and counterfeiter of the truth. He is one who comes as "an angel of light" to offer mankind "godhood" (you are divine and the master of your own destiny).

The sad thing about all this is that these experiences are so real and convincing. People experiencing the superconscious testify that deep meditative states are incomparably beautiful and rapturous. They experience intense light flooding them, and have a sense of omnipotent power and infinite wisdom. In this timeless state, they experience an ecstasy compared to nothing they have ever known before. They feel a sense of unity with all of life and are convinced of their own immortality. Such experiences keep them returning for more. One is not going to *believe* he or she is God if one doesn't *feel* like God.

New Age leader Peter Caddy relates an incident in which a group of Christians confronted him and tried, as he put it, to "save my soul." He told them to come back

and talk to him when they've had the same wonderful
mystical experiences he has had. The point he was trying
to make was that these "naive" Christians had no idea
what the metaphysical life is all about and if they did,
they would want what *he had* rather than trying to convert
him to *their* way of thinking.

Feelings such as this are common in New Age circles
and have hooked many over the past twenty years. They
feel something this great *has* to be of God. A similar
account is related in Acts 8:9-11:

> But there was a certain man, called
> Simon, which beforetime in the same city
> used sorcery, and bewitched the people of
> Samaria, giving out that himself was some
> great one: To whom they all gave heed,
> from the least to the greatest, saying, This
> man is the *great power of God.* And to
> him they had regard, because that of long
> time he had bewitched them with sor-
> ceries (italics mine).

In the Greek, the word *bewitched* means to "amaze"
or "astound." *Sorcery* means using the power of familiar
spirits. What this man was doing had to have appeared
good, otherwise the people would not have felt that "this
man is the great power of God." The truth of the matter is,
he wasn't of God, it just appeared that way.

In light of all this, it is easy to see why the coming of
the Christian gospel to Ephesus, that bastion of the
Ancient Wisdom, had such a dramatic effect.

And many that believed came, and
confessed, and shewed their deeds. Many
of them also which used *curious arts*
brought their books together, and burned
them before all men: and they counted the
price of them, and found it fifty thousand
pieces of silver. So mightily grew the
word of God and prevailed (Acts 19:18-
19, italics mine).

The word *curious* is translated from a Greek word
meaning "magical." The magical or metaphysical arts
went out the door when the Gospel of Christ came in. The
two were not only *incompatible*, but *totally opposite* as
the following account reveals:

And when they were at Salamis, they
preached the word of God in the syna-
gogues of the Jews: and they had also
John to their minister. And when they had
gone through the isle unto Paphos, they
found a certain *sorcerer, a false prophet,* a
Jew, whose name was Barjesus: Which
was with the deputy of the country,
Sergius Paulus, a prudent man; who called
for Barnabas and Saul, and desired to hear
the word of God. But Elymas the sorcerer
(for so is his name by interpretation) with-
stood them, seeking to *turn away the
deputy from the faith.* Then Saul, (who
also is called Paul,) filled with the Holy
Ghost, set his eyes on him, and said, O
full of all *subtility* and all *mischief,* thou

> *child of the devil,* thou *enemy of all righ-*
> *teousness,* wilt thou not cease to *pervert*
> *the right ways of the Lord?* (Acts 13:5-10,
> italics mine).

A DISTINCT DIVISION

If you feel (as many New Agers do) that Jesus' real
teachings were suppressed and distorted, then consider
this: Jesus was a good Jew who strictly adhered to what
we now call the Old Testament. In the Old Testament, as
we have seen, contact with familiar spirits (spirit guides)
was strictly forbidden. King Saul is a prime example of
what happened to those who ignored this taboo.

> So Saul died for his transgression
> which he committed against the Lord,
> even against the *word of the LORD,*
> *which he kept not,* and also for asking
> counsel of *one that had a familiar spirit,*
> to inquire of it. And inquired not of the
> Lord: therefore He slew him, and turned
> the kingdom unto David the son of Jesse
> (1 Chronicles 10:13-14, italics mine).

Also in Judaism, there was a distinct division between
God and man as the following verses indicate:

> Ye are my witnesses, saith the Lord,
> and my servant whom I have chosen: that
> ye may know and believe me, and under-
> stand that I am He: *before me there was*
> *no God formed, neither shall there be*

*after me. I, even I, am the Lord; and
beside me there is no saviour.* I have
declared, and have saved, and I have
shewed, when there was no strange god
among you: therefore ye are my witness-
es, saith the Lord, that I am God (Isaiah
43:10-12, italics mine).

Thus saith the Lord, thy redeemer, and
He that formed thee from the womb, I am
the Lord that maketh all things; that
stretcheth forth the heavens *alone*; that
spreadeth abroad the earth *by myself*
(Isaiah 44:24, italics mine).

In view of this, Jesus *could not* have been a purveyor
of the Ancient Wisdom and a devout Jew as well. In the
Jewish religion there is *one* Creator/Sustainer and man is
not Him. He *created* man to worship and give glory to
Him. This view also remains the basis for the Christian
view of God.

Jesus' claim to divinity was based on His
Messiahship, a uniquely *Jewish* concept, *not* compatable
with the Ancient Wisdom teachings of human divinity.
He told the Samaritan woman "...salvation is of the Jews"
(John 4:22).

To those who have embraced metaphysics as the truth
of the universe and the way of salvation, let me say this. I
know you are sincere. I know metaphysics makes you
feel good about yourself. I know you have rejected "old-
paradigm" Christianity as unsuitable. But please give serious consideration to Jeremiah 10:6,11.

Forasmuch as there is *none like unto thee, O Lord*; thou art great, and thy name is great in might. Thus shall ye say unto them, the gods that *have not made the heavens and the earth,* even they *shall perish from the earth,* and from under these heavens" (italics mine).

THE FOLLY OF THE AGES

In 2 Corinthians 1:9, the apostle Paul says, "But we had the sentence of death in ourselves, that we should not trust in ourselves, but in God which raiseth the dead." The verse does not say that we should trust in ourselves who are God—it says that we should *not* trust in ourselves but *trust in God.* God is a personal Being, not the "Universe," not a spirit guide, and most certainly *not* humanity.

The reason the New Age is wrong is that it takes devotion, trust, and glory *away* from the One who created us and gives it to man and the rebellious familiar spirits who deceive man into self-glorification. An analogy of this would be an artist's canvas or paint taking credit for the painting rather than the artist.

That is why the Gentile nations were separated from the true God. They were the metaphysicians of old (the Mystery Schools) "who changed the truth of God into a lie, and *worshipped* and served [honored] the *creature* [man] more than the *Creator* [God], who is blessed forever. Amen" (Romans 1:25, italics mine).

This folly was due to the same error that millions are making right now. They turned to the realm of familiar spirits for guidance just as people are doing today.

There is one account in particular that brings out what I want to convey. It is found in Acts 16:16-19.

> And it came to pass, as we went to prayer, a certain damsel possessed with a *spirit of divination* [familiar spirit] met us, which brought her masters much gain by soothsaying [psychic predictions]: The same followed Paul and us, and cried, saying, 'These men are the servants of the most high God, which shew unto us the way of salvation.' And this did she many days. But Paul, being grieved, turned and said to the spirit, 'I command thee in the name of Jesus Christ to come out of her.' And he came out the same hour. And when her masters saw that the hope of their gains was gone, they caught Paul and Silas, and drew them into the market-place and unto the rulers (italics mine).

These verses show four things that are *critical* to understanding the nature and aim of the New Age movement:

> 1. The spirit was the *source* of her power, *not* some latent faculty inherent in the human makeup. When it went, her ability was *gone*.
> 2. The spirit was accurate to a high degree. Otherwise she would not have brought her masters "much gain." You don't become a success with a poor show-

ing.

3. Paul and the spirit were *not on the same side*. This is quite evident by the fact that he cast it out of her.

4. Most important of all, the spirit tried to *identify itself with God*. When it followed Paul and Silas, it was saying the truth, "These men show us the way of salvation." By doing this, the spirit could continue its practice of deceiving all concerned and perhaps later undo what Paul had accomplished.

These spirits are doing the same thing today. This girl, no doubt, believed that it was her "inner divinity" giving her the information that was so effective in "aiding" the community. The truth of the matter is, when you say you have connected with your "inner divinity" and that you are "God," sadly, you have joined the ranks of those who, "Professing themselves to be wise [knowing the truth], they became fools [absurd], and changed the glory of the *uncorruptible* God into an image made like to *corruptible* man" (Romans 1:22-23, italics mine).

Swami Muktnanda was one of the most admired and respected New Age leaders during the 1970's and early 1980's. He was thought by many to be the virtual embodiment of the "God-realized" master. He told His disciples, "Kneel to your own self. Honor and worship your own Being. Chant the mantra always going on within you. Meditate on your own self. God dwells within you as you."[10]

When Muktnanda died in 1983, one of his closest followers revealed that his master "ended as a feeble-minded, sadistic tyrant luring devout little girls to his bed every night with promises of grace and self-realization."[11] Without realizing he was echoing the truth of the verses just quoted, he concluded:

> There is no absolute assurance that enlightenment necessitates the moral virtue of a person. There is no guarantee against the weakness of anger, lust, and greed in the human soul. The enlightened are on an equal footing with the ignorant in the struggle against their own evil.[12]

It is very clear that the metaphysical explosion that our society is currently awash in is a continuation of what Leviticus 19:31 warned against: "Regard not them that have familiar spirits, neither seek after wizards [metaphysicians], to be *defiled* by them: *I am* the Lord your God" (italics mine).

On this basis alone, Christians have a duty to challenge the validity of the New Age message that *we* are "God."

CHAPTER 9

The End of the Age

The subject covered in this chapter has traditionally been called the "Apocalypse" or the end of the age. In the Bible it is referred to as "the Day of the Lord." Bible scholars refer to it as the time of "the Great Tribulation." This time begins when the Lord Jesus Christ comes to catch away true believers in Him. The apostle Paul describes it for us in 1 Thessalonians 4:16-17.

> For the Lord Himself shall descend from heaven with a shout, with the voice of the archangel, and with the trump of God: and the dead in Christ shall rise first: Then we which are alive and remain shall be *caught up* together with them *in the clouds*, to meet the Lord *in the air:* and so shall we ever be with the Lord (italics mine).

He also spoke of this event prophetically in 1 Corinthians 15:51-55.

> Behold, I shew you a mystery; We shall not all sleep, but we shall all be changed, in a moment, in the twinkling of an eye, at the last trump: for the trumpet shall sound, and the dead shall be raised incorruptible, and we shall be changed. For this corruptible must put on incorrup-

tion, and this mortal must put on immortality. So when this corruptible shall have
put on incorruption, and this mortal shall
have put on immortality, then shall be
brought to pass the saying that is written,
Death is swallowed up in victory. O death,
where is thy sting? O grave, where is thy
victory?

This has been the hope of believers in Christ Jesus
since those words were written. Believers who are alive
during this event will fulfill the promise, "Death is swallowed up in victory."

During this time the one Christians refer to as the
"Antichrist" will make his appearance. The Bible refers to
this personality as "the Son of Perdition," "the Man of
Sin," and "the Wicked One." He will unite the world
under a *counterfeit* spiritual system that blasphemes God
and His plan.

We read in Revelation 13:5-6:

And there was given unto him a
mouth speaking great things and blas-
phemies; and power was given unto him
to continue forty and two months. And he
opened his mouth in blasphemy against
God, to blaspheme His name, and His
tabernacle, and them that dwell in heaven.

Ultimately, this impostor will be knocked from power
by the *literal* Second Coming of Jesus Christ at the end of
the seven-year tribulation period. Second Thessalonians
2:8-10 tells us:

> And then shall that Wicked be
> revealed, whom the Lord shall consume
> with the spirit of His mouth, and shall
> destroy with the *brightness of His com-
> ing*: Even him, whose coming is after the
> working of Satan with all power and signs
> and lying wonders, And with all deceiv-
> ableness of unrighteousness in them that
> perish; because they received not the love
> of the truth, that they might be saved (ital-
> ics mine).

After the destruction of this deceiver and his false program, the true Savior (Jesus Christ) sets up His kingdom on Earth and rules for 1,000 years. This period of time is referred to as the Millennium, a time when *true* rest and peace takes place on the Earth.

THE TIMES AND SEASONS

In light of these prophecies. the advent of the New Age movement takes on a very special significance.

The apostle Paul spoke of the Day of the Lord in reference to "the times and seasons" in 1 Thessalonians 5:1-2.

He was making reference to the Old Testament book of Daniel. King Nebuchadnezzar had a dream concerning the Gentile kingdoms which would begin with his kingdom, Babylon, and continue through Media-Persia, Greece, Rome and a future ten kingdoms. Before Daniel interpreted the dream he made it known that God is responsible for the changes in dispensations which he called "the times and seasons."

> Daniel answered and said, 'Blessed be
> the name of God for ever and ever: for
> wisdom and might are His: And
> *He changeth the times and the seasons:*
> He removeth kings, and setteth up kings:
> He giveth wisdom unto the wise, and
> knowledge to them that know understand-
> ing: He revealeth the deep and secret
> things: He knoweth what is in the dark-
> ness, and the light dwelleth with Him'
> (Daniel 2:20-22, emphasis added).

When asked by the Apostles in Acts 1:6 whether God
would restore the kingdom at that time (bringing in the
millennium), Jesus replied in verse 7, "*It is not for you to
know the times or the seasons.*" It is very apparent that
this phrase is connected to changes in dispensations. In
light of this, study the verses in 1 Thessalonians 5:1-9
very carefully where the apostle Paul states:

> But of the *times and the seasons,*
> brethren, ye have no need that I write
> unto you. For yourselves know perfectly
> that the day of the Lord so cometh as a
> thief in the night. For when they shall say,
> Peace and safety; then sudden destruction
> cometh upon them, as travail upon a
> woman with child; and they shall not
> escape. *But ye, brethren, are not in dark-
> ness, that that day should overtake you
> as a thief.* Ye are all the children of light,

and the children of the day: we are not of
the night, nor of darkness. Therefore let us
not sleep, as do others; but let us watch
and be sober (italics mine).

Paul is saying that the end of the age will come upon
the world like a thief in the night—it will sneak up on
people. Then he contrasts two groups. "But *ye* brethren
[followers of Christ], are not in darkness [ignorance] that
that day should overtake *you* as a thief [unaware]" (v. 4).
He is saying that believers in Christ will have the information available to them to prepare for "that day."

Paul goes on to say, "Ye are all the children of light,
and the children of the day" (v. 5). Those who walk in the
light can see both where they are going and what is coming ahead. He warns against spiritual slumber and drunk-
enness which could lead to a person being overtaken by
that day unaware. "Therefore let us not sleep, as do others; but let us watch and be sober" (v. 6). The word *sober*
here means "alert" or "aware." If one is instructed to
watch and be aware there must be something to *watch
for*—otherwise, Paul's admonition would be useless. The
reason Paul said, "Ye have no need that I write unto you,"
is because the forewarning of when that day would be
came from Jesus Christ Himself.

COMING IN HIS NAME

My research has brought me to a point where the full
implication of Paul's words are surprisingly real. I believe
the Bible contains an important signal that the changes of
times and seasons may indeed be at hand. In Matthew

24:3-5, which is a chapter dealing with the Tribulation period, Jesus spoke these revealing words to His disciples concerning the signs of His coming and the end of the world (age):

> And as He sat upon the mount of Olives, the disciples came unto Him privately, saying, 'Tell us, *when shall these things be?* and what shall be *the sign* [indication] of thy coming, and of the *end of the world* [age]?' And Jesus answered and said unto them, 'Take heed that no man deceive you. *For many shall come in My name, saying, I am Christ; and shall deceive many'* (italics mine).

In the past, I have heard two basic ways of interpreting verse 5 — "for many shall come in my name, saying, 'I am Christ;' and shall deceive many." The first interpretation is that there will be various ones claiming to be the returned Jesus Christ. The other view, which has gained greater acceptance in the last ten or fifteen years, is that a number of messiah figures would appear and gather followers to themselves in a similar fashion to Jim Jones or Bhagwan Shree Rajneesh. I now feel both of these interpretations are incorrect. It is in light of some predominant New Age viewpoints that these verses take on major significance.

A basic tenet of New Age thinking is that of "the Master Jesus." Adherents to this idea believe that during the unrecorded period of His life, Jesus traveled to various occult centers and Mystery Schools in such places as

Tibet, India, Persia, and Egypt where He learned the metaphysical secrets of the ages. Thus, they claim He spent seventeen years of travel on a pilgrimage of higher consciousness. According to this theory Jesus of Nazareth became the "Master" Jesus, one who has gained mastery over the physical world by becoming one with his Higher Self.

You will recall that one of the terms that New Agers regularly use for the Higher Self is the "Christ consciousness." To them, Christ is not a person, but a state-of-being. Excerpts from the following New Age sources explain it this way:

> ...Jesus Christ educated His followers to discern the real man. He taught that there is a power in man that gives him authority over the things of the world. This principle is the higher self, the spiritual man, the Christ.[1]

> The Christ Consciousness or Christ Principle represents the idea of a Savior, but not, as taught in orthodox religions, a physical, material person. Jesus became the Savior as He rose to the heights of His inner powers and became a True Son of God. In other words, when Jesus, the man, was ready, the Christ Principle or Consciousness took over and predominated.[2]

After reading innumerable such statements in New
Age material, I decided to take a closer look at Matthew
24:5. What I found astounded me. The Greek word for
many in this verse is "polus" which means a "very great"
or "sore" number, as in millions and millions. A term
derived from this word is "hoi polloi," which translates
"the masses." The Greek words for "shall come in my
name" means they shall come claiming to represent what
He represents by using His name or authority. Therefore,
Matthew 24:5 is saying that a *very great* number of people shall come claiming to represent what He represents,
but are in fact, deceiving people. In light of "come in my
name," consider the following remarks taken from a variety of New Age sources.

> Jesus was an historical person, a
> human being; Christ, the Christos, is an
> eternal transpersonal condition of being.
> Jesus did not say that this higher state of
> consciousness realized in him was his
> alone for all time. Nor did he call us to
> worship him. Rather, he called us to fol-
> low him, to follow in his steps, to learn
> from him, from his example.[3]

> Jesus was one soul who reached the
> state of Christ Consciousness, there have
> been many others. He symbolized the
> blueprint we must follow....The way is
> open to everyone to become a Christ by
> achieving the Christ Consciousness
> through walking the same path He

walked. He simply and beautifully
demonstrated the pattern.[4]

The significance of incarnation and
resurrection is not that Jesus was a human
like us but rather that *we are gods like
him*—or at least have the potential to be.
The significance of Jesus is not as a vehi-
cle of salvation but as a model of perfec-
tion.[5]

Jesus was aware of himself as a finished specimen of the new humanity
which is to come—the new humanity
which is to inherit the earth, establish the
Kingdom, usher in the New Age.[6]

This view, then, is that Jesus is a "model" of what the
New Age or Aquarian person is to become. I would say
these statements can be called coming in His name or
claiming to represent what He represents.

Now let us look at the second part of verse 5 in
Matthew 24, "...saying I am Christ." Again, we find a
multitude of statements such as the following:

Every man is an individual Christ; this
is the teaching for the New Age. The
experiences of contacting the Christ Self
and the subsequent vibrational lifting *are
not to be reserved for a favored few.*
Every person in the world, sooner or later,
will receive this lifting action. *No one* will

be left out or left behind. *Everyone* will receive the benefit of this step in *human evolution* (italics mine).[7]

Could it be that many Christians have been looking for "the Christ" in all the wrong places? Could it be that when Jesus said "no man knoweth the hour" of his return, it was because the return of the Christ comes *now*, within us, and is beyond space and time? Jesus may have been hinting at this when he told us that "the kingdom of God is within you"—not in some time, nor in some place, but *within*. When we look within, through meditation and the expansion of consciousness, we move beyond time, and meet face-to-face with the Christ.[8]

The Christ is You. You are the one who is to come—each of you. Each and every one of you![9]

Christhood is not something to come at a point in the future when you are more evolved. Christhood is—right now! I am the Christ of God. You are the Christ of God.[10]

Even more specific evidence ties the New Age into this prophecy. In Luke 21:7-8, we find the same discourse as in Matthew 24:3-5. Again, note the warning:

> And they asked Him, saying, 'Master,
> but when shall these things be? and what
> sign will there be when these things shall
> come to pass?' And he said, 'Take heed
> that ye be not deceived: for many shall
> come in My name, saying, I am *Christ;*
> and the time draweth near; go ye not
> therefore after them' (Luke 21:7-8).

Notice "Christ" is italicized in verse 8, meaning that it
was not in the original manuscript. The translators of the
King James Bible probably thought it awkward that it
said, "Many shall come saying, I am." Probably for the
sake of clarity and to be consistent with Matthew 24, the
translators added the word "Christ." It is very interesting
that New Agers refer to themselves (or their Higher
Selves) as the "I AM," (one of the names of God). Note
the following:

> The first experience of unification
> with the Christ consciousness may come
> with the initial crossing of the psychic
> barrier and contact with the Christ Self or
> I AM Self.[11]

> This Inner Self is called by many
> names such as: God-self, Higher-self,
> Christ Consciousness, I-AM, Buddah
> Nature, and many others.[12]

> This I AM is God...this I AM is
> You...Universe   and   Individual
> Consciousness...God knowing Itself as

God, God knowing Itself as You, and You
knowing Yourself as God.[13]

So what Jesus may have been saying is many shall be
saying "I AM."

Because of these statements I firmly believe what
Jesus Christ was prophesying in Matthew and Luke was
the current New Age movement when it reaches its full
fruition world-wide. He clearly stated that just before His
physical return a huge number of people will proclaim
their own personal divinity and that "many" (polus) will
deceive not some, but "many." There was a good reason
for Him to preface these prophesies with the warning,
"Take heed that no man deceive you. For [because]...."
These people will be offering a spiritual message that will
look, feel, and sound like it is of Jesus Christ but is not.

THE MAN OF SIN

Paul declared that during this time "the Man of Sin,
the Son of Perdition" would proclaim himself to be
"God." One channeled source made it clear that the term
Christ will mean both the "Christ energy" and a man that
will *personify* that energy. Consider the following New
Age statements:

The reappearance of the Avatar [world
teacher], by whatever name he may be
known, has been prophesied in many religions as well as in the esoteric [occult]
tradition. A major manifestation is expect-
ed in connection with the Aquarian age.[14]

[A] Savior appears every two thousand years (more or less) for the different
ages. Each Savior brings the tone or keynote for the age.[15]

Literally, the Second Coming of the
Christ is the discovery within each one of
you, and all of mankind, of his or her
divinity, his or her Christ-hood....The only
thing which will call for "an individual"
representing the Christ appearing on your
planet, will be for those doubting
Thomases, those who refuse to acknowledge their divinity, who have it invested
solely in one man. *They will need one
man to appear who they will listen to,*
who will then turn their attention back on
themselves and get about the business of
waking up! (italics mine).[16]

I believe that this coming Aquarian Messiah will be
the Son of Perdition that 2 Thessalonians speaks of and
that the New Age movement is his *spiritual
platform*—too many things fit together for this to be just a
coincidence.

Daniel 8:23 states that this man will be a master of
"dark" sayings. In Hebrew, this translates as one skilled in
cunning and ambiguous speech. Keep this in mind as you
read the following quote:

The coming one will not be Christian,
a Hindu, a Buddhist, not an American,
Jew, Italian or Russian—his title is not

important, he is for all humanity, to unite
all religions, philosophies and nations.[17]

The only one who would be able to bring something
such as this off is the one who fits the decription of the
person mentioned in Daniel. That is why all this effort to
saturate society with meditation is going on right now.
When this man comes forward, all those who are in touch
with their "Higher Selves" (familiar spirits) are going to
automatically recognize him as "the Coming One" and
give him their allegiance. He will have a ready made con-
stituency, many in key positions, to help him reconstruct
society. This will be the final culmination of the paradigm
shift.

The potential *power* of this deception is keenly
brought out in the following observation made by a disci-
ple of Indian Guru Rajneesh and also reflects what the
Antichrist will do with humanity:

> ...Something had happened to
> Rajneesh that made him unlike other men.
> He had undergone some change—enlight-
> enment, the rising of kundalini—and his
> being had been altered in palpable
> [noticeable] ways. The change in him in
> turn affected his sannyasins [disciples]
> and created a *persistent and catalyzing*
> *resonance between them* (italics mine).[18]

The Bible predicts that the Antichrist shall worship a
"god of forces," and that he will perform "lying wonders."
Alice Bailey described "the Work" of the New Age Christ
very explicitly:

> The work of the Christ (two thousand
> years ago) was to proclaim certain great
> possibilities and the existence of great
> powers. His work when He reappears will
> be to prove the fact of these possibilities
> and to reveal the true nature and potency
> of man.[19]

The following is a prime example of what she is talking about: A 55-year-old Hindu spiritual teacher named
Sri Chinmoy has demonstrated an ability to lift 7,000
pounds *with one arm.* This was witnessed by twenty spec-
tators and recorded by photograph and video. He attributed his impressive ability to "meditation power" and
admits that without it he could not lift 60 pounds.[20]

What enabled him to do this was the power of familiar spirits giving him (and those observing this) the
impression that this was done through the power of his
Higher Self. This is what the Bible means by "lying wonders." The Man of Sin will do this on an even larger scale.
He will seem to work great miracles to show everyone
that they are all "christs" and that they all have this great
"power," or as Bailey said, "potency" within them.

In light of this, consider the following story of a
woman's encounter with a "healer":

> Instantly my body felt as though it
> were filled with white light and I became
> weak in my knees and I started swaying.
> Soon, I became unable to stand, and
> someone helped me to sit in a chair.
> Thereafter, I felt extreme heat beating

down into my head, particularly on the
left side. All during this experience, I was
completely conscious and my body was
filled with waves of ecstasy. It was an
oceanic feeling, much greater than
orgasm, since it involved my whole being.
I remember breathing deeply to support
the increased energy in my system. I was
so happy that I began to moan in pleasure
and then to laugh aloud. I had heard about
and visualized whitelight before, but had
never experienced being totally infused
with it. I immediately made an association
to the healing power of Jesus Christ, and
had *no doubts* that this was the nature of
the energy being transmitted to me.[21]

The man that did this to her was a *New Ager*. This
shows that even known occultists have the power
—through familiar spirits—to mimic what most people
would consider to be of God.

Bailey also revealed: "The ground is being prepared
at this time for the great restoration which the Christ will
engineer." In the context of that statement, she informs us
that what will be restored are "the ancient Mysteries."[22]
These are the same as the Mystery Schools.

The origin of the Antichrist's religious system is
revealed by the apostle John in Revelation 17:5:

And upon her forehead was a name
written, **Mystery, Babylon the Great, the
mother of harlots and abominations of
the earth.**

Another word for Babylon in the Old Testament was Chaldea. The Chaldeans were renowned for their use of the metaphysical arts. They were the first Mystery School. Daniel 4:7 says, "Then came in the magicians, the astrologers, *the Chaldeans,* and the soothsayers." The Old Testament book of Leviticus makes reference to those who listen to familiar spirits as "whoring after them," and Deuteronomy 18 refers to the practices of metaphysics as "abominations" in God's sight. This *Mystery Babylon,* then, would be the *original source* or "mother" of what is now New Age metaphysics.

Thus, when John identifies the Antichrist's spiritual format, he is making reference to the city and people that first spawned occultism in ancient times. *All* of the other Mystery Schools came out of Babylon teaching basically the *same thing*—the Ancient *Wisdom.* John saw it as one unbroken line throughout history culminating in Antichrist's rule when hundreds of millions are given over to familiar spirits.

It is the correlation between what the Bible says about the Antichrist and his design and what the New Age says about its intentions that lead me to believe the two are *one and the same.*

THE BLOOD OF THE SAINTS

One of the main tenets of New Age thought is peace, goodwill, and the unity of all humanity. Remember, the Age of Aquarius is to be the "Age of Oneness." In context with this idea, there is evidence supporting what New Agers term as the "cleansing." A number of books make reference to those who are *laggards* when the New Age reaches its maturity.

> Remnants of the Fifth Root Race [untransformed humanity] will continue to survive in the initial stages of the new Cosmic Cycle, but unless they increase their awareness or consciousness to the Higher Mind and the tempo of spirituality, they will be removed from the Life Stream of the Race.[23]

> Unity-motivated souls will respond to His [The New Age Messiah's] call, their inner drive for spiritual world unity will synchronize with higher energy. People opposing the recognition of the Christ may struggle intensely, but it will not be prolonged. The Christ energy by then will be so strong people will be *dealt with* according to their own individualized karma and *their ability and desire to assimilate this accelerated energy* (italics mine).[24]

> ...The final appearance of the Christ will be an evolutionary event. It will be the disappearance of egocentric [lower self], subhuman man and the ascension of God-centered Man. A new race, a new species, will inhabit the Earth—people who collectively have the stature of consciousness that Jesus had.[25]

Those who cannot be awakened will
not be permitted to dwell in this world.
They will be sent to some equally appropriate place to work their way to
understanding.[26]

If one understands the rationale behind these statements, then it becomes clear what they are talking about.
Those who will accept the "Christ consciousness" can
stay—those who won't—*must go*. The quote about people's "desire and ability" to assimilate the "Christ energy"
as the determining factor in their fate is very thought pro-
voking.

You will recall David Spangler's words from Chapter
8, about Lucifer being the angel of man's "inner evolution." Christians know Lucifer to be Satan, the
Adversary, and 2 Thessalonians 2:9 informs us that Satan
is the one who will empower the Antichrist. Those defying the Antichrist will really be defying Satan—and they
will suffer dearly for it.

Persecution and death is *predicted* in the Bible for
those who won't fall into line during the Antichrist's rule.
The parallel between what the Bible says about this period and the statements above are striking. The following
prophecies reveal what is in store for those who will
preach the *real* Jesus Christ and the Gospel of the *true*
kingdom during this time. Jesus said in Matthew 24:9,
"Then shall they deliver you up to be afflicted, and *shall
kill you:* and ye shall be hated of all nations for my
name's sake" (italics mine). "They" are the many who are
coming in His name claiming to be "christs."

Revelation 6:9-10 says of this period:

And when He had opened the fifth
seal, I saw under the altar the souls of
them that were *slain for the word of God,*
and for the testimony which they held:
And they cried with a loud voice, saying,
'How long, O Lord, holy and *true*, dost
thou not judge and avenge *our blood* on
them that dwell on the earth?' (italics
mine).

Revelation 20:4 says:

And I saw thrones, and they sat upon
them, and judgment was given unto them:
and I saw the souls of them *that were*
beheaded for the witness of Jesus, and
for the word of God, and which had not
worshiped the beast, neither *his image,*
neither had received his mark upon their
foreheads, or in their hands; and they
lived and reigned with Christ a thousand
years (italics mine).

The following verse lends credence that this will be
on an individual spiritual basis: "And ye shall be betrayed
both by parents, and brethren, and kinfolks, and friends;
and some of you shall they cause to be put to death"
(Luke 21:16). This implies that a family member or a
friend may be turned over to be dealt with "for their own
good." It will be seen as an altruistic act. New Agers
never say that *they* are going to "remove" anybody—it is

inferred that this will be done by "natural causes."
Was Hitler a forerunner of this? Quite possibly. The
swastika, the main symbol of Nazism, is an age-old
Hindu symbol that is still found on many temples
throughout India. The word is not even German, but
Sanskrit—Svastika—meaning "that which is excellent."[27]
A New Age book has described its meaning as representing "the final stage in which the chakras are active, developed, open, and energized by awakened kundalini energy."[28] Thus, the very banner of Nazism stood for the
energy that underlies the whole New Age movement.
New Agers even acknowledge this. David Spangler
makes reference in one of his books to "...the Nazi movement, which had many roots in occultism."[29] The swastika symbol was also prominently displayed on Madam
Blavatsky's personal brooch, in exactly the same style as
the Nazi one (tilting at an angle to the right) decades
before the Nazi Party was even formed. One can also see
the parallel between Nazism and the Ancient Wisdom in
the Hindu caste system, with its Brahmin (aryan) caste
and its lower "untouchable" caste. The Nazis also took
the term Aryan—literally, "the worthy race"—from
Hinduism.[30] The word has nothing to do with ancient
Germany as many believe, but is a Hindu word meaning
noble or superior.

IS THE CHURCH SPIRITUAL ISRAEL?

It states in Matthew 24:14 that "the gospel of the
kingdom shall be preached in all the world" during those
seven years. This is the message that the Antichrist will
try to stamp out with all his might. Those who preach the

message that Jesus Christ is coming to set up His kingdom are the ones who will be killed.

In Luke 21:8, the Lord tells His disciples that when "many" come claiming to represent His character saying, "I am Christ," or "I am God," then the time of His coming will be close. When "the time" does come, the Lord will come back with "power and great glory" (v. 27) and "as a snare" (v. 35). His kingdom comes upon "the whole earth" (v. 35). The Man of Sin (Antichrist) is then unseated and destroyed by "the brightness of His [Christ's] coming" (2 Thessalonians 2:8). Then the kingdom will be established in Israel as promised. See Ezekiel 36:22-38 and 43:1-9.

One fact concerning Bible prophesy is quite clear. When Jesus Christ returns to set up the kingdom of heaven, it is the *Antichrist* who has had "dominion" over the earth the previous seven years—*not* the Body of Christ. Before the Man of Sin comes to power, the Body of Christ will be taken out, caught up in the clouds, gathered together, or "collected" as one concordance refers to it.

Some people believe that the church is "spiritual Israel" and all promises made to national or ethnic Israel now apply to the Body of Christ. But according to Revelation 7:2-4, this cannot be the case. It says:

> And I saw another angel ascending from the east, having the seal of the living God: and he cried with a loud voice to the four angels, to whom it was given to hurt the earth and the sea, Saying, 'Hurt not the earth, neither the sea, nor the trees, till we have sealed the servants of our God in

their foreheads.' And I heard the number
of them which were sealed: and there
were sealed an hundred and forty and four
thousand of *all the tribes of the children
of Israel* (italics mine).

In verses five through eight the tribes are then named.
If the church is now spiritual Israel, what "spiritual" tribe
does a Christian belong to? The answer is *none* because
these verses are talking about ethnic Jews who will
preach the true Gospel of the real kingdom. In Luke 1:31-
33 the angel Gabriel told Mary:

And, behold, thou shall conceive in
thy womb, and bring forth a son, and shall
call His name Jesus. He shall be great,
and shall be called the Son of the Highest:
and the Lord God shall give unto Him
the throne of His father David: And *He
shall reign over the house of Jacob forever;* and of His kingdom there shall be no
end (italics mine).

The "throne of His father David" and the "house of
Jacob" refers to the nation of Israel. In Isaiah 2, it says
"out of Zion [the nation of Israel] shall go forth the law
and the word of the Lord *from* Jerusalem."

CHAPTER 10

Salvation

Second Thessalonians 2:10 talks about those who will follow the Antichrist and participate in his belief system, "And with all deceivableness of unrighteousness in them that perish; because they received not the love of the truth, that they might be saved."

WHO WILL BE AMONG "THEM THAT PERISH?"

Ephesians 1:13 makes reference to the "gospel of your salvation." If you have always wondered what church to join or whether you have been "good enough" to get into heaven, then understand that the only thing that really *counts* is whether or not you are a member of the Body of Christ. The way of entering the Body of Christ is by believing the "gospel of your salvation." Let's look into what this entails.

To accept salvation, you have to realize that you *need* salvation. To do that you have to admit something to yourself that is very unpopular these days; that you are an *unrighteous person.* If at first you find this idea offensive and unacceptable, then consider the qualifications for being unrighteous.

Being filled with all unrighteousness, fornication, wickedness, covetousness, maliciousness; full of envy, murder, debate, deceit, malignity; whisperers,

backbiters, haters of God, despiteful,
proud, boasters, inventors of evil things,
disobedient to parents, without understanding, covenant breakers, without natural affection, implacable, unmerciful:
Who knowing the judgment of God, that
they which commit such things are worthy of death, not only do the same, but
have pleasure in them that do them
(Romans 1:29-32).

This means if you have ever in your life:

...been greedy
...made trouble for someone
...been jealous of anybody for *any* reason
...gotten mad at or argued with someone because
    they did not agree with you
...lied to cover up your wrongdoing or to get some-
    thing
...played a dirty trick on someone
...gossiped or said bad things about others
...broken a promise or a deal
...bragged about yourself
...looked down on anyone
...been stubborn on settling an issue
...lacked compassion towards someone
...done other activities of this kind, or even been
    sympathetic with someone else doing them, then
    you are *unrighteous*. These things do not apply in
    just extreme cases but common, everyday
    instances too.

CAN WE BE RIGHTEOUS BEFORE GOD?

Jesus Christ gave the requirements to be counted righteous before God in and of yourself in Matthew 22:37-40:

> Jesus said unto him, 'Thou shalt love the Lord thy God with all thy heart, and with all thy soul, and with all thy mind. This is the first and great commandment. And the second is like unto it, Thou shalt love thy neighbor as thyself. On these two commandments hang all the law and the prophets.'

That means you would have to love God and everybody around you *exactly* as you love yourself. That might be easy to do as long as everything went your way, but when conflict or adversity arose, things would get a little difficult. This would also have to be something you *successfully did your entire life*, not just *tried* to do. Hardest of all, you would have to do this not only in *deed* but also in *thought* because "Man looketh on the outward appearance, but the Lord looketh on the heart" (1 Samuel 16:7).

If we loved everyone as we love ourselves we would not be *capable* of the sins mentioned earlier. People love *themselves* first and foremost. This is the reason why the world is in such bad shape. Not only is this evident in our daily lives and the lives of those around us, but it is also a pronouncement of the Bible, "For all have sinned, and come short of the glory of God" (Romans 3:23). Again in Romans 3:10, "As it is written, There is none righteous [innocent], no, not one."

If you disagree with these verses, then answer this question: Would you mind having *all* your inner thoughts and fantasies revealed to everyone you know? I am sure, if you reflect on that possibility for any length of time, you would find it most unacceptable.

GOOD WORKS OR GRACE

The New Age and Christianity definitely disagree on the answer to this dilemma of human imperfection. Metaphysics puts forth the doctrine of reincarnation and karma where the soul, through good works,evolves through many "lives" to a point where it can free itself from earthly bondage and become Self-realized, united with the "universe," which is seen as God, but in reality is the realm of familiar spirits.

On the other hand, the gospel Christians embrace offers salvation to mankind through *grace* (unmerited favor). Romans 3:24 says, "Being justified freely by His grace through the redemption that is in Christ Jesus." Then in Romans 6:23 we read, "For the wages of sin is death; but the gift of God is eternal life through Jesus Christ our Lord."

This "gift" is not earned or given as a reward for earnest effort or good intentions. Ephesians 2:8-9 states clearly, "For by grace are ye saved through faith; and that not of yourselves: it is the gift of God: Not of works, lest any man should boast."

The reason human effort does not work is because man is "...dead in trespasses and sins" (Ephesians 2:1). The word *works* is translated "actions" or "doings." This can either mean good deeds or engaging in religious rituals. In metaphysics, the very word *karma* translates to mean "actions" or "works." By your own effort and doings you are supposed to advance spiritually. If you are "dead" spiritually, as the Bible states, the concept of karma would be like trying to start a car without a battery.

NEW AGE'S CLASH WITH CHRISTIANITY

Where Christianity and the New Age clash most decidedly is in the nature of the person and work of Jesus Christ. The New Age sees Him as a great master, a way-shower to "Christ-consciousness," a metaphysical guru—someone who is the prototype of the Aquarian Age man.

The way Christians see Him can be summed up in the verses in John 20:31, "But these are written, that ye might believe that Jesus is the Christ, the Son of God; and that believing ye might have life through His name," and in Hebrews 2:9, "But we see Jesus, who was made a little lower than the angels, for the suffering of death, crowned with glory and honor; and He by the grace of God should taste death for every man." This verse reveals to us that Christ's sacrifice for all mankind is the ultimate act of love.

Accepting this act of love is how man is justified before God: "In whom we have *redemption through His blood*, the forgiveness of sins, according to the riches of His grace" (Ephesians 1:7, italics mine). Romans 5:9-10 goes on to explain, "Much more then, being now *justified by His blood,* we shall be saved from wrath through Him. For if, when we were enemies, we were reconciled to God by the *death of His Son,* much more, being reconciled, we shall be saved by His life" (italics mine).

As we read earlier in Ephesians 2:8, "For by grace are ye saved through *faith*..." It is faith in the sacrifice of Jesus Christ as it pertains to you *personally* that is the key element in the "gospel of your salvation."

THE BAD NEWS AND THE GOOD NEWS

Do you wonder why God set such high standards that can't possibly be fulfilled by mankind? Well, the bad news is that there is *nothing* you can do about your sinfulness. But the good news is that, as you have already read, there is nothing you *have* to do except believe that God's grace is sufficient for you. Grace is God doing for man what man is unable to do for himself—not man doing for God.

Romans 4:4-5 explains, "Now to him that worketh is the reward not reckoned of grace, but of debt. But to him that worketh not, but believeth on Him that justifieth the ungodly, his faith is counted for righteousness." This is "the simplicity that is in Christ" (2 Corinthians 11:3).

If you still believe that Jesus Christ is your *model* rather than your *Savior* and that you can attain the same level that He did, then you would also have to...

> ...have been born of a virgin (Isaiah 7:14, Matthew 1:18)
> ...tell someone their whole life history without ever having met them and not be wrong (John 4:28-29)
> ...raise the dead (Matthew 9:24-25)

...raise yourself from the dead (Matthew 16:21;
John 2:19-21)

...create and uphold the material universe
(Colossians 1:16-17) and specifically be *head of
the church* (v. 18), and the *King of Israel* (Acts
2:29-30, Luke 1:32)

...come back to earth at the head of a mighty host
and have every knee bow and have every tongue
confess that *you are Lord* (Philippians 2:10-11

...most important of all, were you to truly follow
Christ's example, you would die for the sins of
the whole world and by your death the whole
world would have redemption through *your
blood.*

Those New Agers who see themselves as "christs"
have not "tasted death for every man" nor can anyone
have redemption through *their* blood. Through their meditation experiences they have been deceived into believing it is their "Christ-selves" that they are in touch with.

FAITH IN WHAT?

Simply believing that there is a God will not be satis-
factory either. If there is a personal God, then you must
deal with Him on a personal level. Many people are religious but their faith is misdirected.

A friend of mine, who is a member of the Body of
Christ, was visiting his parents. His mother, who was an
elder in a prosperous suburban protestant church, asked
him whether he was saving his money, or not. He told her

that he felt the Lord was returning soon and that saving money was not one of his prime goals.

Displeased at what she heard, his mother began to chide him for his remark. In return he asked her,

> "What do you believe in, Mom?"
> "I have *faith*, Larry, I have *faith*," she replied.
> "In *what*, Mom?"
> "I have faith in *my church* and *human nature*," she proudly proclaimed.

It is sadly apparent that this woman, despite her Christian background, already had one foot in the New Age, as millions like her must also have.

This view is backed up by some recent data. One source revealed:

> While religion is highly popular in America, it is to a large extent superficial; it does not change people's lives to the degree one would expect from their level of professed faith. Related to this is a "knowledge gap" between Americans' stated faith and the lack of the most basic knowledge about that faith.[1]

In the spring of 1991, New York University released a nationwide study which showed 86% of all Americans identified with Christianity. Yet, another recent study showed that only 19% of Americans knew that being a Christian was having a *personal* relationship with Jesus Christ.[2]

They have not grasped what "the gospel of your salvation" is all about—which can be summed up by the following verses:

> This is a faithful saying, and worthy
> of all acceptation, that Christ Jesus came
> into the world to save sinners; of whom I
> am chief (1 Timothy 1:15).
> But not as the offense, so also is the
> free gift. For if through the offense of one
> many be dead, much more the grace of
> God, and the gift by grace, *which is by
> one man, Jesus Christ,* hath abounded
> unto many (Romans 5:15, italics mine).

Notice again the verse says, "by *one man.*" Salvation is having personal faith and trust in the *person* and *finished work* (sacrifice) of the Lord Jesus Christ. We have "peace with God" (Romans 5:1), are "forgiven" (Ephesians 5:4), and are "reconciled" to God (2 Corinthians 5:18) only by *Him.* That's where our faith or trust is to be directed.

The notion of achieving "Christ consciousness" is just not *compatible* with being redeemed by Christ's precious blood. The two just don't mix. Romans 5:6 says, "For when we were yet without strength [spiritually impotent], in due time Christ *died* for the ungodly."

A "consciousness" can't die for anyone—only a *person* can. The decision you make on this issue will determine whether or not you will be among those who "receive not the love of the truth that they might be saved." John 4:24 says, "God is a Spirit: and they that

worship Him *must* worship Him in spirit and in truth"
(italics mine).

GOD'S DESIRE

"For this is good and acceptable in the sight of God
our Savior; Who will have all men to be saved, and to
come unto the knowledge of the truth" (1 Timothy 2:3-4).

> In whom ye also trusted, after that ye
> heard the word of truth, the gospel of
> your salvation: in whom also after that ye
> believed, ye were sealed with that holy
> Spirit of promise (Ephesians 1:13).

It is God's desire that none should perish eternally.
That's why he offered His Son, the Lord Jesus
Christ—the only perfect sacrifice for mankind's sin.

What it comes down to is the preaching of the
"Higher Self" versus "the preaching of the cross." The
New Age is saying that God is the Higher Self in
man—that God is just a meditation away.

Many people are turned off to the Christian teaching
that we are bad and worthless. *Not so.* It may teach that
man is bad (which is evident) but certainly not worthless.
The fact that Christ *died* for the "ungodly" to "reconcile"
them to God shows God's love toward man. In contrast,
the gospel of Grace is better than karma in that if you
accept its provision, you are complete (perfect) in Christ
Jesus.

This is why Christianity is so steadfast on these

issues. If a belief system is not the preaching of the cross, then it is not "the power of God" (I Cor. 1:18). If other ways are correct, then Christ died in vain, His blood *unnecessary*.

STILL SKEPTICAL?

If some readers still feel what I'm talking about is irrational or off-track then take notice of the following. In 2nd Peter 3:8, the context being the end of the age, Peter reveals that:

> But, beloved, be not ignorant of this one thing, that one day is with the Lord as a thousand years, and a thousand years as one day.

In the Old Testament book of Hosea, it informs us:

> "I will go and return to my place, till they acknowledge their offense, and seek my face; in their affliction they will seek me early. Come, and let us return unto the Lord; for he hath torn, and he will heal us; he hath smitten, and he will bind us up. After *two days* will he *revive us;* in the *third day* he will *raise us up,* and we shall *live in his sight"* (Hosea 5:15-6:2, italics mine).

If "I" in verse 15 represents the Lord and "they" are Israel and "their affliction" is the tribulation period, then, in view of Peter's statement the tribulation would be around 2,000 years (or 2 days) after the Lord's resurrection and return to heaven. *On* the 3rd "day" He will return and Israel will "live in His sight."

Bible scholars tell us that it was 4,000 years from Adam to Jesus Christ. It has been almost 2,000 years from Christ to now. In Exodus 31:12-17, it states that the Sabbath, or seventh day was to be a *sign* between the Lord and *Israel.* If the 7th day represents the 7th thousand year period as being the millennial kingdom reign of Christ, then this chronological model *fits right in, for* the Tribulation *must* preceed the millennium.

Isaiah 47 gives us another strong indication that this could be the fulfillment of prophecy. In this chapter the "daughter of Babylon" or offspring of the first mystery school is being punished for saying in her heart, "I AM" (verse 8) and practicing "sorceries" (verse 9).

Isaiah then presents a challenge:

> Stand now with thine enchantments, and with the multitude of thy sorceries, in which thou hast labored from thy youth, if so be thou shalt be able to profit, if so be thou mayest prevail. Thou art wearied in the multitude of thy counsels. Let now the astrologers, the stargazers, the monthly prognosticators, stand up, and save thee from these things that shall come upon thee (Isaiah 47: 12).

The next verse (14) reveals that "they" shall be subjectd to great heat. Turn to Revelation 16:8-9 to see who "they" are:

> And the fourth angel poured out his
> bowl upon the sun, and power was given
> unto him to scorch men with fire. And
> men were scorched with great heat, and
> blasphemed the name of God, who hath
> power over these plagues; and they
> repented not to give Him glory.

Back to Isaiah 14 it states that great *cold* comes next. Turning again to Revelation 16 we find:

> And the fifth angel poured out his
> bowl upon the throne of the beast, and his
> kingdom was full of darkness; and they
> gnawed their tongues for pain, and blas-
> phemed the God of heaven because of
> their pains and their sores, and repented
> not of their deeds.

These verses suggest that it is the *Ancient Wisdom* that is being punished during the Tribulation period because its adherents are claiming to be "God." This will be the ultimate test revealing who the *real* God is. If you don't already, I pray you *will* come to know the *true* Christ before it is too late.

> **I AM GOD!** This is **THE** most basic
> tenant of metaphysical spiritual under-
> standing...
>   Metaphysical Teacher[3]

...Jesus calls us to creativity and our own unique I AMness.

John Bradshaw[4]

For thou hast trusted in thy wickedness; thou hast said, 'None seeth me'. Thy *wisdom* and thy *knowledge*, it hath *perverted thee*; and thou hast said in thine heart, 'I *am,* and none else beside me' (Isaiah 47:10).

He that hath the Son [*not* higher consciousness] hath life; and he that hath not the Son of God hath not life (I John 5:12).

Glossary

Ancient Wisdom
The supposed "laws of the Universe" that, when mastered, enable one to control one's own reality. Another word for metaphysics or occultism.

Aquarius/Aquarian Age
Sign of the Zodiac represented by the water carrier, "Earth Age" associated with this astrological sign. (See New Age)

Alice Bailey
British-born occultist who wrote under the guidance of a familiar spirit and channeled nineteen books on the New Age. She also popularized the term.

Blavatsky, H.P.
Russian noblewoman who founded the Theosophical Society in 1875, to spread occultism to western society.

Centering/Centering Prayer
Another term for meditation (going deep within your "center"). A type of meditation being promoted in many mainline churches under the guise of "prayer."

Chakras
Believed by New Agers to be the seven "energy centers" in man which "open up" during the kundalini affect in the individual.

Christ-Consciousness
Thought by New Agers to be the state of awareness, reached in meditation, in which one realizes that one is divine and "one with God" and thereby becoming a "Christ" or an enlightened being.

Crystals
Used by New Agers to enhance their experiences during meditation and store energy for various uses.

Creative Visualization
Imaging in the mind what you want to occur during meditation and then expecting it to happen. In simple terms, you are creating your own reality.

Guru
Master of Metaphysics who teaches students how to attain their optimal spiritual level.

Higher Self
Supposed God-Self within that New Agers seek to connect with through meditation. Also called the Christ-Self.

Holistic or Wholistic
Body/mind/spirit considered as an inseparable unit.

Human Potential
Term used by many in the New Age movement to promote the idea that untapped mental and spiritual resources lie within every person and these can be utilized through various altered-state exercises.

Karma
Literally means "doing;" one's actions. Always linked with the concept of Reincarnation. It means if one's actions are good, one is born into better circumstances in subsequent lives; if one's actions are bad, the opposite is true. This is supposed to promote right living.

Kundalini
Powerful energy that is brought on through meditation, associated with the Chakras.

Mantra
Word or words repeated either silently or verbally to induce an altered state.

Meditation
The practice of stilling and emptying the mind by concentrating on a single point (breath, mantra, candle, etc.) so one may be able to contact spiritual entities such as the "Higher Self" or spirit guides

Metaphysics
The supposed science of dealing with unseen realities (the Spiritual Worlds or Planes) and using these skills to empower oneself to create the desired reality.

New Age
The Age of Aquarius, supposedly the Golden Age, when man becomes aware of his power and divinity.

New Thought
Movement that tries to merge classic occult concepts with Christian terminology.

Occult/Occultism
Kept secret or hidden, the practice of metaphysics throughout history.

Psychic
A person able to obtain information through metaphysical perception.

Reiki
Spiritual energy that is channeled by one attuned to the Reiki power. Literally translated God-energy.

Reincarnation
Spiritual evolution of the soul based on one's Karma or actions.

Self-Realization
Full contact with the Higher Self resulting in "knowing" one's self to be "God."

Theosophical Society
Organization founded by Helena P. Blavatsky in 1875, to spread the Ancient Wisdom (i.e., occultism) throughout western society. The forerunner of the modern New Age movement.

Transpersonal
New Age term which means "beyond the personality;" that which pertains to the Higher Self. Common usages include transpersonal psychology or transpersonal education.

Wicca
Popular term for modern-day witchcraft. Nature religion based on metaphysical practices.

Footnotes

CHAPTER 1

1. "The Spiritual Revolution," *Wholistic Living News,* Vol. 8, Issue 3, (December 1985/January 1986), p. 15.

2. Marion Weinstein, *Positive Magic: Occult Self-Help,* (Custer, Washington: Phoenix Pub., Inc., 1978), p. 19.

3. Anthony J. Fisichella, *Metaphysics: The Science of Life,* (St. Paul, Minnesota: Llewellyn Pub. 1984), p. 28.

4. Weinstein, *Positive Magic,* op. cit. p. 25.

5. Neville Drury, *Dictionary of Mysticism and the Occult,* (San Francisco: Harper and Row Pub., 1985), p. 179.

6. Celesté G. Graham, *The Layman's Guide to Enlightenment,* (Phoenix: Illumination Pub., 1980), p. 13.

7. Ananda's Expanding Light, *Program Guide,* (April-December 1991), p. 5.

8. Barbara Strauss, *What Is Metaphysics?,* booklet.

9. "Yoga, Meditation, and Healing: A Talk with Joseph Martinez," *Holistic Health Magazine,* (Winter 1986), p. 9.

10. "The Joys and Frustrations of Being a Healer," *Life Times Magazine,* Vol. 1, Number 3, p. 59.

11. Swami Rama, *Freedom From the Bondage of Karma,* (Glenview, Illinois: Himalayan International Institute of Yoga Science and Philosophy of U.S.A., 1977), p. 66.

12. Diane Stein, *The Woman's Spirituality Book,* (St. Paul, Minnesota: Llewellyn Pub., 1987), p. 140.

13. Ibid. pp. 141-142.

14. John Randolph Price, *The Superbeings,* (Austin, Texas: Quartus Books, 1989), p. 100.

15. Barbara Marx Hubbard, *Manual for Co-Creators of the Quantum Leap,* (Gainsville, Florida: New Visions), pp. vi-23.

16. *Light of Mind Catalog,* Issue 17, p. 4.

17. Shirley MacLaine, *Dancing In the Light,* (New York: Bantam Books, 1985), p. 350.

18. Kathy Zook, "Card Readings: May Be More Than Luck of the Draw," *The News Guard,* (Lincoln City, Oregon, February 4, 1987), Section C, p. 1.

19. Celesté G. Graham, *The Layman's Guide to Enlightenment,* op. cit. p. 55.

CHAPTER 2

1. George Trevelyan, *A Vision of the Aquarian Age,* (Walpole, New Hampshire: Stillpoint Pub., 1984), p. 161.

2. 1981 Gallup Poll.

3. C. William Henderson, *Awakening,* (New Jersey, Prentice Hall, 1975), p. 213.

4. *Eugene Register Guard,* (Eugene, Oregon: March 16, 1984).

5. "Mystics on Mainstreet," *U.S. News and World Report,* (February 9, 1987), p. 69.

6. Geoffrey Parrinder, *World Religions from Ancient History to the Present,* (New York: Facts on File Pub., 1971), p. 155.

7. Charles J. Ryan, *What is Theosophy? A General View of Occult Doctrine,* (Point Loma Pub., Inc., 1975), p. 16.

8. Colin Wilson and John Grant, *The Directory of Possibilities,* (New York: The Rutledge Press, 1981), p. 50.

9. Harold Balyoz, *Three Remarkable Women,* (Flagstaff, Arizona: ALTAI Pub., 1986), pp. 191, 205, 207.*

10. Ibid. p. 207.

11. Ibid. p. 210.

12. Ibid. p. 217.

13. Alice A. Bailey, *The Externalization of the Hierarchy,* (New York: Lucis Pub. Co., 1957), p. 604.

14. Ken Cary, *The Starseed Transmissions,* (Uni-Sun Pub., 1982), pp. 3-4.

15. Ibid. pp. 31-32.

16. Bryant Reeve, *The Advent of the Cosmic Viewpoint,* (Amherst, Wisconsin: Amherst Press, 1965), p. 260.

17. "Eine Bewegung Hebt Ab," (A movement takes off), *Tempo Magazine,* (December 12, 1986), pp. 45-46.

18. Robert Adams, *The New Times Network,* (London: Routledge, Kegan, Paul, 1982), p. 117.

19. Peter Spink, *Spiritual Man in a New Age,* (London: Darton, Longman and Todd, Ltd., 1980), p. 45.

*Information taken from *The Unfinished Autobiography* by Alice Bailey, (Lucis Pub. Co. New York, 1951).

20. Gale Worner and Michael Shuman, *Citizen Diplomats,* (New York: Continuum Pub.), pp. 195-196, 200.

21. Sharon E. Mumper, "Where in the World is the Church Growing?" *Christianity Today,* (July 11, 1986).

22. Bryant Reeve, *The Advent of the Cosmic Viewpoint,* (Amherst, Wisconsin: Amherst Press, 1965), p. 259.

23. "Lazaris," *Concept:* Synergy, Promotional Flyer, (Fairfax, California).

24. Shirley MacLaine, *Out on a Limb,* (New York: Bantam Books, 1983), p. 312.

25. David Spangler, *Emergence: The Rebirth of the Sacred,* (New York: Dell Publishing Company, 1984), p. 67.

26. Talk by Ken Carey at Whole Life Expo, (Los Angeles: February, 1987).

27. Kathleen Vande Kiefr, *Innersource: Channeling Your Unlimited Self,* (New York: Ballantine Books, 1988), p. 38.

28. J.L. Simmons, *The Emerging New Age,* (Santa Fe, Bear and Co., 1990), p. 211.

29. Ibid. p. 13.

CHAPTER 3

1. "Bottom-Line Intuition," *New Age Journal,* (December 1985), p. 32.

2. "What's New in the New Age?" *Training Magazine,* (September 1987), p. 25.

3. *Science of Mind,* (May 1983), pp. 11-12.

4. "From Burnout to Balance," Interview with Dennis Jaffe, Ph. D., *Science of Mind,* (June 1985), pp. 88-89.

5. Michael Ray and Rochelle Meyers, *Creativity in Business,* (Garden City, New York: Doubleday and Company, Inc., 1986), front cover.

6. Ibid. back cover.

7. Ibid. back flap.

8. Ibid. pp. 36-37.

9. Ibid. p. 142.

10. Ibid. p. 154.

11. Craig R. Hickman and Michael H. Silva, *Creating Excellence, Managing Corporate Culture Strategy, and Change in the New Age,* (New York: New American Library, 1984), Preface.

12. Ibid. p. 116.

13. "The Megatrends Man," *Newsweek,* (September 23, 1985), p. 61.

14. John Naisbitt and Patricia Aburdene, *Reinventing the Corporation,* (New York: Warner Books, 1985), p. 139.

15. Ibid.

16. "Wellness Works: A New Lifestyle for a New World," Interview with Elaine Willis, Ph.D., *Science of Mind,* (June 1990), p. 25.

17. Ibid. pp. 19-20.

18. *Science of Mind,* (June 1988), p. 77.

19. "Changing the Game in Business," Interview with Larry Wilson, *Science of Mind,* (February 1987), p. 10.

20. Ibid. p. 14.

21. Ibid. p. 88

22. Willis Harmon, "The New Age of Consciousness," *Guide to New Age Living,* (1989), pp. 18, 20.

23. "Disciples of the New Age," *International Management Magazine,* (March, 1991), p. 45.

24. Larry Wilson, op. cit. p. 31.

CHAPTER 4

1. Marilyn Ferguson, *The Aquarian Conspiracy,* (Los Angeles: J.P. Tarcher, Inc., 1980), p. 280.

2. Ibid. p. 281.

3. Promotional Flyer, *Self-Esteem Seminars,* (Pacific Palisades, California).

4. "Education In The New Age," Interview with Jack Canfield, Ph.D., *Science of Mind,* (December 1981), p. 11.

5. *Self-Esteem,* op. cit.

6. *Science of Mind,* (December 1981), p. 108.

7. Gay Hendricks and Russell Wills, *The Centering Book,* (Englewood Cliffs, New Jersey: Prentice-Hall, Inc., 1975), pp. 169-171.

8. Storma Swanson, *Attuning to Inner Guidance,* (Beaverton, Oregon: Seabreeze Press, 1982), p. 3.

9. Ibid. p. 16.

10. David B. Ellis, *Becoming a Master Student,* (Rapid City, South Dakota: College Survival, Inc., 1985), front page.

11. Ibid. p. 27, 30.

12. Ibid. p. 134.

13. The Learning Annex, Seattle Center, (October 1987), pp. 7, 11.

CHAPTER 5

1. "Healing Hands," *New Woman Magazine,* (March 1986).

2. Dennis Livingston, "Balancing Body, Mind, and Spirit," *1988 Guide to New Age Living,* p. 17.

3. Robert Hass and Cher, *Forever Fit,* (New York: Bantam, 1991), p. 165.

4. Ormand McGill, *Hypnotism and Meditation,* (Glendale, California: Westwood Publishing Company, 1981), p. 68.

5. *New Woman,* op. cit. p. 78.

6. "The Reiki Touch," *The Movement Newspaper,* (October 1985).

7. Barbara Ray, Ph.D., *The Reiki Factor,* (St. Petersburg, Florida: Radiance Associates, 1983), p. 65.

8. "Vincent J. Barra Psychic Healer Transmits Reiki Energy," *Meditation Magazine,* (Summer 1991), p. 31.

9. "The Mysterious Healing Power of Reiki," *East-West Journal,* (November 1985), p. 53.

10. Paula Horan, *Empowerment Through Reiki,* (Wilmot, Wisconsin: Lotus Light Pub., 1990), p. 9.

11. Bodo J. Baginski and Shalila Sharamon, *Reiki Universal Life Energy,* (Mendocino, California: Life Rhythm, 1988), pp. 33, 49-50.

12. "Sharings," *The Reiki Journal,* Vol. VI, No. 4, (October/December 1986), p. 17.

13. "The Potentials of Therapeutic Touch," Interview with Janet F. Quinn, Ph.D., R.N., *Science of Mind,* (May 1988), p. 14.

14. Ibid. p. 83.

15. Ibid. p. 83-84.

16. Ibid. p. 87.

17. *The Truth About Crystal Healing,* (St. Paul, Minnesota: Llewellyn Pub., 1987), p. 9.

18. *Magical Blend Magazine,* Issue 14, p. 14.

19. Barbara Ann Brennan, *Hands of Light,* (New York: Bantam, 1987), p. 187.

20. Ibid. p. 182.

21. Ibid. p. 182.

22. *USA Weekend Sunday Supplement,* (July 24-26, 1987), p. 12.

23. Lazaris on the "Merv Griffin Show," *Concept: Synergy,* (Fairfax, California: Synergy Productions, 1986), p. 2.

24. "The Many Faces of Keven Ryerson," *Yoga Journal,* Issue 69, (July/August 1986), p. 28.

25. "Two Billion People for Peace," Interview with John Randolph Price, *Science of Mind,* (Aug. 1989), p. 24.

26. Kathleen Vande Kieft, *Innersource: Channeling Your Unlimited Self,* (New York: Ballantine Books, 1988), p. 114.

27. Laurie Cabot, *The Power of the Witch,* (New York: Dell, 1989), p. 173.

28. "Cosmic Consciousness: The Ultimate Joy," Interview with Jack Addington and wife, *Science of Mind,* (July 1983), p. 32.

29. Zolar, *Zolar's Book of the Spirits,* (New York: Prentice Hall Press, 1987), p. 227.

30. Betty Bethards, *Way to Awareness: A Technique of Concentration and Meditation,* (Novato, California: Inner Light Foundation, 1987), p. 23.

31. Ken Wilber, "The Pundit of Transpersonal Psychology," *Yoga Journal,* Issue 76, (September/October 1987), p. 43.

32. "Music, Stress, and Your Health," Interview with Steve Halpern, *Science of Mind,* (February 1989), p. 14.

33. Ibid. p. 15.

34. Joy Lake Seminar Center, 1988 Catalog, p. 43.

CHAPTER 6

1. "Is There a New Age Answer to Drug Abuse?" *Cycles Magazine,* (March 1987), p. 13.

2. John Bradshaw, *Bradshaw on the Family,* (Pompono Beach, Florida: Health Communications, 1988), p. 235.

3. John Bradshaw, *Healing the Shame That Binds You,* (Pompono Beach, Florida Communications, 1988), p. 222.

4. John Bradshaw, *Bradshaw on the Family*, op. cit. p. 229.

5. Bradshaw, *Healing the Shame*, op. cit. p. 230.

6. *Leading Edge Review*, (Holiday 1990), front cover, and p. 11.

7. Steven Halpern, promotional mailer.

8. Melody Beattie, *Co-dependent's Guide to the Twelve Steps*, (New York: Prentice Hall, 1990), p. 179-180.

9. Ibid. pp. 262-265.

10. Ibid. pp. 187-188.

11. Robin Norwood, *Women Who Love too Much*, (New York: Pocket Books, 1986), p. 236.

12. Ibid. p. 291.

13. Joel S. Goldsmith, *Practicing the Presence*, New York: Harper and Row Publishers, 1986), pp. 95, 97-98.

14. Norwood, *Letters From Women*, op. cit. p. 345.

15. Robert Handly with Pauline Neff, *Anxiety and Panic Attacks*, (New York: Fawcett Crest, 1985), p. 139.

16. Ibid. pp. 214-215.

17. Ibid. p. 216, 217.

18. "Discoveries Through Inner Quests," *Gateways Institute*, (Fall 1988), p. 2.

19. Ibid. p. 5.

20. Ibid, pp. 2, 19, 21.

21. "Awaken to Your Unlimited Potential," *Potentials Unlimited Inc.*, p. 23.

22. Ibid.

23. Ibid. p. 24.

24. *Light of Mind Catalog*, Issue 17, (Light of Mind Pub.), p. 6.

25. *Reflections Resource Directory*, (Portland, Oregon: Fall 1986), p. 16.

26. "Meeting Your Inner Guide," article in publication put out by local New Age bookstore.

27. Ibid.

28. Jacqueline Small, *Transformers: Therapists of the Future*, (Marina del Ray, CA: De Vorss and Co., Publishers, 1982), prologue, p. xiii.

CHAPTER 7

1. Keating, Pennington, and Clarke, *Finding Grace at the Center,* (Still River, Massachusettes: St. Bede Pub., 1978), pp. 5-6.

2. Anthony de Mello, S.J., *Sadhana: A Way to God,* (X. Diaz del Rio, S.J., Gujarat Sahitya Prakash, Anand, Gujarat. 388 001, India, 1978), pp. 3-4.

3. Ibid. p. 9.

4. Ibid. p. 15.

5. *Wake Up to Life,* (St. Louis, Missouri: We and God Spirituality Center), p. 2.

6. Ibid.

7. Harvey D. Egan, S.J., Quoted on back cover of *Sadhana,* (Catholic Theological Society of America, Proceedings - XXXV, 1980), p. 104.

8. Benjamin Walker, *The Hindu World,* Vol. 11, M-2, (New York: Frederick A. Praeger Pub., 1968), p. 394.

9. James Finley, Michael Pennock, *Your Faith and You,* (Notre Dame Ind.: Ave Maria Press, 1978), p. 394.

10. Chilson, *Full Christianity,* (Paulist Press, 1985), p. 136.

11. *San Francisco Sunday Punch,* (March 8, 1987).

12. *Science of Mind,* (June 1988), p. 77.

13. Richard E. Geis' personal journal, "The Naked Id."

14. "New Age Isn't New to Salem," *Statesman Journal* newspaper article, Salem, Oregon, (March 9, 1991), p. 2-A.

15. M. Scott Peck, M.D., *The Road Less Traveled,* (New York, Simon and Schuster, Inc., 1978), pp. 269-270.

16. "Peck's Path to Inner Peace," *Newsweek,* (November 18, 1985), p. 79.

17. Ibid.

18. Barry A. Ellsworth, *Living in Love With Yourself,* (Salt Lake City: Breakthrough Pub., 1988), back cover.

19. Mathew Fox, *The Coming of the Cosmic Christ,* (San Francisco: Harper and Row, 1988), back cover.

20. Philip Busuttil, "Hard Love," *New Age Journal,* (December 1985), pp. 30-31.

21. Promotional Flyer for *The Spiritual Growth Institute,* (Eugene, Oregon).

22. Ken Carey, *The Starseed Transmissions,* (Uni-Sun Pub., 1982), p. 33.

23. David Spangler, *Emergence: The Rebirth of the Sacred,* (New York: Dell Pub. Co., 1984), p. 112.

24. M. Basil Pennington O.C.S.D., *Centered Living the Way of Centering Prayer,* (New York: Bantam Books, 1986), p. 192, 193-194.

CHAPTER 8

1. Shakti Gawain, *Creative Visualization,* (California: Whatever Pub., 1978), pp. 48, 56, 91, 93.

2. Yott, *Man and Metaphysics,* (New York: Weiser, 1980), p. 110.

3. James S. Gordon, *The Golden Guru,* (Lexington, Maine: The Stephen Greene Press, 1987), p. 8.

4. Yott, *Man and Metaphysics,* op. cit. p. 110.

5. Gawain, *Creative Visualization,* op. cit. p. 15.

6. David Spangler, *Reflections on the Christ,* (Findhorn Foundation, 1977), p. 36.

7. Ibid. p. 41.

8. "Reiki, The Healing Touch," *Life Quest Magazine,* (May/June 1988), p. 25.

9. Barbara Ray, Ph.D., *The Reiki Factor,* (St. Petersburg, Florida: Radiance Assoc., 1983), p. 129.

10. "Kundalini Demystified," *Yoga Journal,* Issue 64, (September/October 1985), p. 43.

11. "Baba Beleaguered," *Yoga Journal,* Issue 63, (July/August 1985), p. 30, (reprinted from CoEvolution Quarterly, Winter 1983).

12. Stan Trout, excerpts from an open letter, *Yoga Journal,* Issue 63, (July/August 1985), p. 30.

CHAPTER 9

1. *Metaphysical Bible Dictionary,* (Unity Village, Missouri, Unity School of Christianity).

2. Donald H. Yott, *Man and Metaphysics,* (New York: Weiser, 1980), p. 73.

3. John White, "Jesus, Evolution, and the Future of Humanity," *Science of Mind Magazine,* (September 1981), p. 15.

4. John Davis and Naomi Rice, *Messiah and the*

Second Coming, (Wyoming, Michigan: Coptic Press, 1982), p. 49.

5. White, *Science of Mind,* (October 1981), pp. 40-42.

6. White, *Science of Mind,* (September 1981), p. 15.

7. Armand Biteaux, *The New Consciousness,* (Oliver Press, 1975), p. 128.

8. Gregory Barrette, "The Christ is Now," *Science of Mind,* (March 1989), p. 17.

9. *Life Times,* Vol. 1, No. 3, p. 91.

10. John Randolph Price, *The Planetary Commission,* (Austin, Texas: Quaratus Books, 1984), pp. 143, 145.

11. Anne P. and Peter V. Meyer, *Being a Christ,* (San Diego: Dawning Pub., 1975), p. 49.

12. John Baughman, *The New Age,* (Self-Published, 1977), p. 5.

13. Price, *The Planetary Commission,* op. cit. p. 98.

14. Simons Roof, *About the Aquarian Age,* (The Mountain School of Esoteric Studies), p. 7.

15. Yott, *Man and Metaphysics,* op. cit. p. 74.

16. *Life Times,* Vol. 1, No. 3, p. 90.

17. Davis and Rice, *Messiah and the Second Coming,* op. cit. p. 150.

18. James S. Gordon, *The Golden Guru: The Strange Journey of Bhagwan Shree Rajneesh,* (Lexington, Massachusetts: The Stephen Greene Press, 1987), pp. 235-236.

19. Alice A. Bailey, *The Reappearance of the Christ,* (New York: Lucis Publishing Company, 1948), p. 124.

20. Lynn Scott, "Sri Chinmoy Lifts Over 7,000 Pounds with One Arm," *Life Times Magazine,* Vol. 1, No. 3, p. 45.

21. Marjorie L. Rand, "Healing: A Gift That Awakens," *The Whole Person,* (June 1988), p. 40.

22. Bailey, *The Reappearance of the Christ,* op. cit. p. 121.

23. Yott, *Man and Metaphysics,* op. cit. p. 58.

24. Davis and Rice, *Messiah,* op. cit. p. 152.

25. John White, "The Second Coming," *New Frontier Magazine,* (December 1987), p. 45.

26. B.J. Williams, "Head Trip," *Northwest Magazine,* (Portland, Oregon: Sunday Oregonian, August 9, 1987), p. 9.

27. Geoffrey A. Barborka, *Glossary of Sanskrit Terms* (Buena Park, California: Stockton Trade Press), p. 64.

28. Zachary F. Lansdowne, Ph. D., *The Chakras and Esoteric Healing,* (York Beach, Maine: Samuel Weiser, Inc., 1986), p. 159.

29. David Spangler, *Emergence: The Rebirth of the Sacred,* (New York: Dell Publishing Company, 1984), p. 114.

30. Barborka, op. cit. p. 15.

CHAPTER 10

1. George Gallup, Jr. and Jim Castelli, *The People's Religion,* (New York: MacMillan Pub., 1989), p. 21.

2. George Barna, *The Frog in the Kettle,* (Ventura: Regal Books, 1990), p. 114.

3. "I AM," Communicated through Kathy Wilson, *The Light of Olympia Newspaper,* Vol. 1, Number 8, (August 1988), p. 7.

4. John Bradshaw, *Homecoming: Reclaiming and Championing Your Inner Child,* (New York: Bantam Pub., 1990), p. 274.

Personal Relationship
by Thomas LeBlanc

Christianity is not a religion, but a relationship – a living personal relationship with God. He desires to be a real part of our lives. He longs to develop a personal relationship with each of us.

In this book, you will read about many examples of how Jesus can touch and influence a person's life. You will see that only He can eliminate our guilt and fill our emptiness. Learn how through Him, we can overcome fear. You will understand that He offers a peace that surpasses human comprehension.

In this book you will:
- Learn how "emptiness" is filled
- See how to combat fear
- Understand God's peace
- Recognize God's faithfulness
- Discover the ingredients for a miracle

New Discovery:
- Learn how our thoughts and words affect our physical bodies.

Thomas LeBlanc is a Christian businessman, a registered physical therapist and a publisher. He has authored Christian tracts, a physical therapy article, and an electronic communications text that is used in technical colleges across the country. He lives with his wife, Karen, and three children, in Oregon.

Available from

Solid Rock Books, Inc.
979 Young Street, Suite E
Woodburn, Oregon 97071
(503)981-0705

Other products from Solid Rock Books, Inc. include:

☑ **Books**

☑ **Audio Tapes**

☑ **Video Tapes**

For a *FREE* catalog, please write to:

Solid Rock Books, Inc.
979 Young Street, Suite E
Woodburn, Oregon 97071
(503)981-0705